# Evangelicalism in Mexico City

## Religious Differentiation and Structural Change (2014-2015)

Marco Ornelas

First English Edition, 2018.

This book is the English translation of post-doctoral research done in Universidad Iberoamericana during 2014-16 and published as: Ornelas, Marco. 2016. *Evangélicos en la Ciudad de México (CDMX). Diferenciación religiosa y cambio estructural (2014-2015)*. Saarbrücken: Editorial Académica Española.

Cover: The Last Angel (1912) by Nicholas Roerich. Nicholas Roerich Museum, New York. (www.roerich.org)

Edition and English Translation by the Author.
Mexico City, 2018.

# Contents

This research began as a study of Pentecostals in Mexico City which in its own right was extended to various evangelical groups. The comparative perspective with traditional Catholicism that has predominated in these lands –and with the structural change which accompanies it, tendentially unfavorable to Catholicism– became evident from the beginning. The history of modern Pentecostalism presented here must be taken in the sense of an unfinished sketch which outline hypotheses to be developed, rather than as a Definitive History of world Pentecostalism. However partial and incomplete it may appear, what is clear is that Mexico has not been able to escape from it (and here I refer strictly to historical sources).

If a timeline were to be drawn for this exercise, it would have to start in the year 1875 with the Christian charismatic revival at the Keswick Convention (Cumbria, England), it would necessarily pass through Pandita Ramabai's Mukti revival in Kedgaon (Maharashtra, India ) from 1896, would have to incorporate the revivals in Topeka, Kansas (1900) and that of the Azusa Street in Los Angeles, California (1906) in the United States, would include the revival in the Methodist Church of Valparaiso, Chile (1909), and end up driving into northwest Mexico (Villa Aldama, Chihuahua) in the midst of the Mexican Revolution in 1914. As we will have opportunity to see, a timeline is an important help but also –unavoidably– a caricature of planetary highly complex sociocultural evolutionary processes.

The fundamental characteristic of the investigation –which is not necessarily its success: everything depends on the eye with which we look at it– is the interdependence of social systems theory with "the realities" it gives shape to and even with the way of naming them. Sociological theory and social and cultural historical narratives are accomplices of each other. In addition to social theory and historiography, the study contains census information and fieldwork (participant observation) in six evangelical churches in Mexico City.

The work intends to re-phrase religious differentiation in a Mexican key. In this sense, this research is the legitimate daughter of *Modern Religious Differentiation: The Latin Mass (1517-1570)*, recently published (2018) independently through Amazon.com, and it could even be said that constitutes its continuation. It is worth insisting that basic research and its possible application yields are separated by many years in distance. The study that follows counts as an application of social systems theory to the analysis of the social structure and semantics of contemporary world society.

Marco Ornelas

6

# 1. Introduction: The Sociological Study of Religions

This chapter does not intend to fully develop the central concepts of Luhmann's sociology of religion, although it will make use of some basic notions which allow to clarify the particular interpretation made here of statistics of religious membership. For those interested in exploring the sociology of religion of Niklas Luhmann they can turn to Luhmann (1998, 2007a, 2007b, 2009).

Luhmann addresses religions *exclusively* as communication, and even rites and doctrines are nothing but forms of religious communication. In his words, when religion is the subject matter, the matter is "exclusively religious communication, religious meaning which is actualized in communication as the meaning of communication" (Luhmann 2007b, 37).[1]

Religions, thus, are considered here as a communicative phenomenon and, as such, as an event which is difficult to circumscribe in a particular territory. This means that religious communications are related to space in a wide-spread manner. This is why it was necessary to propose a concept that was able to show this circumstance and allow for this particular theoretical turn to take place. The concept is that of *religious resonance* and it takes over the place of the traditional "religious membership". Religious resonance indicates the population percentage which

---

[1] All translations into English are the author's responsibility.

declares belonging to some denomination,[2] given the assumption of an existing world religious communication system.[3]

## Mexico: A Space for the Study of Religious Communication

Religious resonance, in this sense, always implies the *interpenetration*[4] (Luhmann 1998, 199-235) between the world religious communication system –represented by religions

---

[2] The question in the census is: Which is Peter's religion? Compare http://www.inegi.org.mx/est/contenidos/proyectos/aspectosmetodologicos/cuestionarios/default.aspx. (June 10, 2014).

[3] This would be the most obvious and immediate consequence of using this concept. Another one –the most important for its theoretical implications– would be that religious resonance indicates the impact of religious communication in the internal societal environment, that is, the benefit of religion on other social systems. On the concept of resonance, compare Luhmann (1989).

[4] For an example of how non-conformist Christian communication interpenetrates –a special case of structural coupling– Martin Luther, the beginner of the Reformation, compare Ornelas (2018b). For a definition of structural coupling compare what follows.

available to the population at any time–, and the psychological system of human beings (the conscious, discriminative faculty of individuals in a territory). Religious resonance supposes the selection done by populations among denominations available in the world religious communication system or, put differently, the selection of religions "*à la carte*" (Luhmann 2007b, 250-251).

This research assumes that there is now a single world society (Luhmann 2007a, 11-12). The other major assumption of social systems theory, which separates it from other sociological theories, is that world society is *communicatively differentiated* in such a way that no communications system has a preponderance over any other (Stichweh 2015). World society is a heterarchical society, that is, a society without a center. This world society is composed of world-wide communications systems (economy, politics, law, art, religion, science) which operate semantically closed –the concept that designates this feature is that of *autopoiesis*–. Social systems have their own binary codes, for example, the binary code transcendence/ immanence of religious communications (Luhmann 2007b, 49 ff).

*Programs* of different social systems (Luhmann 1989, 44 ff) indicate the rules with which one can legitimately communicate according to a particular reference code. For example, for the program of Christian Pentecostal communications it is about transcendental communication when the baptism of the Holy Spirit has been received through, among other events, the gift of tongues. Glossolalia, then, can only be fully incorporated into the program of Pentecostal Christianity through its consideration as "baptism of the Holy Spirit".

The semantic closure of different social systems occurred unevenly and was related to diverse events, largely contingent, whose examination is the center of the theory of *sociocultural evolution* (Luhmann 2007a, 325ff). Modern society supposes the co-evolution of social systems in the way of communicative specialization and autonomization. The operational closure of different social systems took place in a space of several centuries. As examples, the closing of the religious system began with the Protestant Reformations of the sixteenth century (Luhmann 2009, 164ff, 272ff), the art system began its closure during the Renaissance (Luhmann 2005, 223ff), and the political system turned into an autopoietic one by the end of the French revolution of the late eighteenth century (Torres Nafarrate 2004, 380ff). In general it can be said that world society became such, always in a partial and gradual way, starting from the fifteenth century. At the end of the eighteenth century this evolutionary process concludes with world society as we know it today.

Different social systems operate in parallel and in operational closure conditions, and never the relationship between them is simple, direct. Rather, the way in which social systems relate to each other is through *structural couplings* (Luhmann 2007a, 66ff, 615ff). Structural couplings are not only supposed among different social systems, but also between communications, consciousness and organisms of human beings. The particular case of structural coupling between communications and consciousness is referred to by the theory with the concept of interpenetration (Luhmann 1998, 199ff). On this basis, one can have a better image of the hyper-complexity of world society.

In an epistemological and methodological level it could be said that social systems theory is a radical constructivist theory of observation (Luhmann 1996, 335ff). The bases of this development have their origin not only in Philosophy (Edmund Husserl) and in Sociology (Talcott Parsons), but also in conceptual adaptations coming from Neurobiology (*The tree of knowledge: the biological bases of human understanding* by Humberto Maturana and Francisco Varela, 1984), Mathematics (*Laws of Form* by George Spencer-Brown, 1969) and Second-order cybernetics (*Observing Systems* by Heinz von Foerster, 1981).

If the operations of social systems are composed of nothing more than communications, all communication *temporalization* must be conceived before anything else as an artificial sequence of communication. This means that the sequence is built in a somewhat arbitrary way, hence precisely its character of *history* (Luhmann 1998, 90ff). This consideration should not be overlooked, particularly since this study rehearses a world-wide, planetary observation of the history of modern Pentecostalism.

## 1.1 Religious Resonance and Programming: A Cumulative Model of Structural Change

As stated above, contemporary world society works communicatively speaking under conditions of semantic closure. This means that the relationship between different social systems (religion, politics, law, science) is never simple and straightforward. The concept of religious resonance, besides being equated with membership or religious affiliation, refers precisely to the type of relationship presupposed by the theory between different social systems, that is, the relationship of a system with its internal societal environment (for example the relationship of religious communications with political, legal or scientific communications).[5] Transparency or the simple translation of communications between social systems is discarded in principle by the theory.[6] So one could say that religious resonance −as well as that of any other social system− is always limited.

Otherwise, the form of relationship between different types of communications is complex, meaning by this that every system is always under pressure to select information from the environment so that it can be processed as own communication. The binary code of a social system, such as the transcendence/ immanence

---

[5] Compare Luhmann (1989) in special chapters 4 and 9 (Resonance and Codes, Criteria, Programs).

[6] In its place the theory postulates the concept of structural coupling.

code of the system of religion,[7] closes semantically the system with respect to other types of communications. It is only through system programs by which the system of religion is sensitized (it is "open") to environmental information. Programs, it could be said, predispose the environmental information relevant to the system. In this regard, the programs of social systems can be understood as the set of conditional rules (of the type: if, then...) which establishes the ways in which one can legitimately ascribe communication to the system, according to its reference binary code.

Each Christian communication program (Catholic, Orthodox, Protestant Evangelicalism) establishes conditional rules of its own in order to decide whether one is properly dealing with Christian transcendental communication. While some evangelical communications could emphasize the gift of tongues to assert that they deal with transcendental communication (conceived as "baptism of the Holy Spirit"), Catholic communications could alternatively emphasize the importance of sacramental confession or marriage (conceived as "ecclesiastically sanctioned marriage and forgiveness") to indicate that one is effectively dealing with Catholic transcendental communications.

Whence comes the importance of the programs of the religious system to address the issue of the relationships it establishes with

---

[7] Compare Luhmann (2007b, 49ff).

other social systems... in a particular historical setting. Binary codes as well as programs of social systems are the product of historical development and of evolution. The theory of social systems provides a gross approximation to the moment when the semantic closure of several systems began: the Protestant Reformations of the sixteenth century to the system of religion, the Italian Renaissance to the art system, the French Revolution and the drafting of the first European Constitutions for the systems of politics and law, Newtonian physics and the foundation of the Royal Society of London for the system of science.[8]

Religious change is understood as a "cumulative model" of structural change (Stichweh 2008), that is, as a long-term change which involves the gradual modification of expectations. This change could also be understood as "cultural hybridism" (Burke 2010) or as a gradual *mestizaje* or creolization process. This means that religious change is primarily a historical process by which new religious programs are introduced in a new cultural setting, such as those of evangelical Protestantism in traditional Catholic countries like Mexico, which incorporate new elements (adult baptism, baptism by full immersion in water in the name of Christ only, the gift of tongues, physical [laying on hands], emotional and spiritual [exorcism] healing, etc.), while some other elements of the traditional Catholic program gradually lose their

---

[8] Compare for religion (Luhmann 2009, 134-186; 272-282), for art (Luhmann 2005, 223-308), for politics (Torres Nafarrate 2004, 135-176; 380-402), for law (Luhmann 2002, 93-179; 301-358), and for science (Luhmann 1996, 195-260; 389-433).

relevance (to go to Mass, sacramental confession and marriage, the anointing of the dying, etc.).

All these practices, of course, outline different ways in which religion relates to society, that is, ways in which religion couples with political communication (Whom should I vote for on election day?), with legal communication (Should same sex legal marriage be allowed?), with educational communication (Is it proper to provide exclusivist religious education in public schools?), with health communication (Should I vaccinate my children against polio or accept blood transfusions?), and with scientific communication (Should I credit the theory of evolution?).

## 1.2 Implant of Evangelicalism in Mexico

As the transcendence/ immanence code of the religious system closes semantically through a historical and evolutionary process, the various programs of Evangelicalism "open" religious communication to the influences of the internal societal environment during the Mexican nineteenth and twentieth centuries. Evangelicalism programs were resolutely implanted and in time became naturalized. We refer to an "implant" because the arrival of Christian Evangelicalism to Mexico had a clear political purpose –to "sow" an opposition to the hegemonic Catholic Church– first under the auspices of the radical liberal group (1857-1877), and later under the revolutionary nationalist government of Lazaro Cardenas (1934-1940).

In this historical analysis and record on the continuity of the implanted Evangelicalism in evangelical Churches visited in Mexico City, the following points should be emphasized:

a) Unlike cultic and doctrinal uniformity of Catholicism,[9] evangelical communications are too fragmented. This is a characteristic feature of Protestant communications which dates back to the sixteenth century, the century when various Protestant Reformations took place and which expresses as religious differentiation;[10]

b) The various programs of Evangelicalism could be understood as framed in a "heated" communicational milieu (highly volatile, with varying degrees of commitment and identity, and frequent organizational schisms), which could be placed on a continuum with rational features in one end, and magical/ charismatic features in the other, as shown in the following summary table:

---

[9] There is awareness of the emergence of a Catholic Charismatic movement which allows cultic exaltations such as songs, interjections and testimonies, though it is also clear that such expressions are subjected to limitations imposed by a highly centralized hierarchy and by an overwhelming dogmatic homogeneity.
[10] Compare again Ornelas (2018b), in special chapter 3.

PROGRAMS OF EVANGELICALISM

Rational <-----------------------------------------------------------> Magical/charismatic

|  | Lutheran | Baptist | Neo-Pentecostal | Pentecostal | Pentecostal | Pentecostal |
| --- | --- | --- | --- | --- | --- | --- |
| Churches | Cristo | Cristiana Remanente | Semilla de Mostaza | Asambleas de Dios | Centro de Convivencia | Centro Pentecostal |
| Foundation Year | 1962 | 1992 | 2005 | 1918 | 1957 | 1979 |
| **Distinctive Theology** | | | | | | |
| Only faith, grace, scripture/Baptism & Eucharist | | | | | | |
| Continuity of Spirit's Gifts (glossolalia, healing) | | | | | | |
| Cessationism | | | | | | |
| Trinitarian baptism | | | | | | |
| Oneness | | | | | | |
| Prosperity/happiness/success | | | | | | |
| **Relations with Evangelicalism in the US** | FLM/ELCA | Master's Academy | Farmington Heights | Assemblies of God | No apparent relation | UPCI |
| **Social Policy** | Progressist | Conservative | Conservative/Fundamentalist | | | |

Source: Own creation on the basis of Evangelismo defeño: Reporte de campo, 2014-2015 (30 de noviembre de 2015).
https://www.academia.edu/19377529/EVANGELISMO_DEFENO_REPORTE_DE_CAMPO_2014-2015
(December 14, 2018)

c) According to the particular program of Evangelicalism, one can distinguish various theological principles (Cessationism, Trinitarian baptism, Oneness [baptism in the name of Christ only], theology of prosperity), ritual specificities (weight of praise during worship, use of video and audio, temple size, extent and manner of the manifestations of the gifts), and forms of organization/ distinctive leadership (Episcopal [Lutheran], Congregationalist [Baptist], Presbyterian, apostolic-charismatic, or some mixed form).

# 2. Religious Differentiation in Mexico

Chapter Abstract

This chapter presents information on religious membership in Mexico to the year 2010, as well as the official available information on registered cult ministers and religious associations. In addition, it proposes a new way of considering data on religious membership within the sociology of religion of Niklas Luhmann, on the basis of the concept of religious resonance. Religious resonance indicates the population percentage that declares belonging to some denomination, given the assumption of an existing world religious communication system. Even though in Mexico Catholic resonance is of 82.7%, there exist no less than 15 denominations different from Catholicism. The statistical analysis presented allows for the sound suspicion of an inflated Catholic resonance in México otherwise called nominal Catholicism.

Before going into the history of the worldwide emergence of Pentecostalism and its implantation in Mexico from the last century, an excerpt will be made to assess the state of religious communications and its characteristic expression in various regions of the country.

## 2.1 Religious Resonance

Table 1 and its graph show the degree of communicative resonance of the Catholic religion and of denominations different to Catholicism in Mexico.[11]

---

[11] In 1910, at the dawn of the Mexican Revolution and before the establishment of the first Pentecostal churches in the country, Bastian (1990a, 138) counted 700 Protestant congregations with seven thousand faithful (Methodist, Presbiterian and

| Table 1. Catholic and Non-Catholic Resonance in Mexico, 1950-2010. | | | | |
|---|---|---|---|---|
| Year | % Catholics | % Non-Catholics | % Dissonant | |
| 1950 | 98.2 | 1.8 | -- | |
| 1960 | 96.5 | 2.3 | 0.6 | |
| 1970 | 96.2 | 2.2 | 1.6 | |
| 1990 | 89.7 | 6.4 | 3.2 | |
| 2000 | 88 | 7.6 | 3.5 | |
| **2010** | **82.7** | **10** | **4.7** | |
| Sources: Author's own creation on the basis of *La diversidad religiosa en México*. XII Censo general de población y vivienda. INEGI. México, 2005. 191 pp. *Panorama de las religiones en México 2010*. INEG. México, 2011. | | | | |

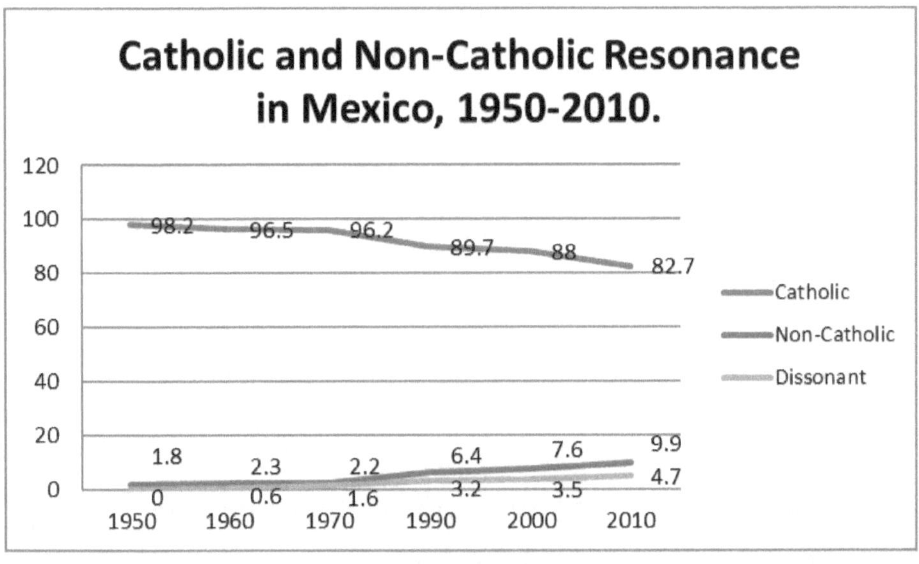



Congregationalists). By then, Mexico's total population was slightly above 15 million. This means that Protestant population did not even reach 0.5% of the total population.

During the second half of the twentieth century, Mexico reduced consistently its Catholic resonance (98.2% to 82.7%), and gave place to an increased resonance of denominations different from Catholicism (1.8% to 9.9%). Another figure of interest: the existence of a visible percentage (4.7%) of religious dissonance, that is, those who do not profess any religion at all.

These data place Mexico within the predominant tendency of world society towards secularization. By secularization is understood not so much the diminished influence of religion in contemporary communications, but above all the relation of religion to the primary form of social differentiation (societal type) in today's contemporary world: the modern or functionally differentiated society (Luhmann 2007b, 241ss). Today, the functionally differentiated or modern society is the primary form of social differentiation in world society, which could be equalized with the differentiation of social communications that led to the specialization of languages (art, science, economics, politics, religion, intimacy).

Is there evidence of a differentiated religious offer in the country and of definite tendencies for an immediate future? Table 2, which presents figures of the main religions in Mexico in chosen states for 2000 and 2010, favors a positive answer. Compared religious resonance for the decade 2000-2010 not only shows the sound fall of the Catholic resonance (88 to 82.7%), but correlates this decrease with increasing numbers of Protestant and Evangelical

(5.2 to 7.5%) and biblical non-Evangelical resonance (2 to 2.3%), and even with the increase of dissonant population (3.5 to 4.7%) – this is not the case of other religions which diminished for the period (0.4 to 0.1%)–.

The national figure is used here as an average against which one can compare the resonance of different religious communications in chosen states. The table presents, besides the national figures, data for two of the most Catholic states in Mexico (Guanajuato and Jalisco), for two of the least Catholic (Chiapas and Tabasco) and for Mexico,[12] Mexico City (CDMX), Nuevo Leon (Nvo Leon), Sonora, Oaxaca, Coahuila, Veracruz, Chihuahua (Chih), Tamaulipas (Tamps) and Baja California (Baja Calif). Apart from Catholic resonance, there exists resonance of Protestant and Evangelical communications (Mennonites, Baptists, of the Nazarene, Methodists, Presbyterians, Evangelicals and Pentecostals), of biblical non-Evangelical communications (Jehovah's Witnesses, Seventh-day Adventists and Mormons [The Church of Jesus Christ of Latter-day Saints]), and of other denominations (of Eastern origin, Judaism, Islam, of ethnic roots, Spiritualism and other). This would be, so to speak, the menu of religions available in Mexico, waiting to be interpenetrated by the population.

---

[12] Besides Mexico City, there is a state in Mexico which is called after the name of the whole country!

# Table 2. Religious Resonance Compared: 2000, 2010.

| Religious Resonance in Selected States, 2000. | | | | | |
|---|---|---|---|---|---|
| States[a] | % Catholic | % Protestant and Evangelical[b] | % biblical non-Evangelical[c] | % dissonant | % other[d] |
| Guanajuato (4049950) | 96.4 | 1.3 | 0.7 | 0.7 | 0.1 |
| Jalisco (5541480) | 95.4 | 2 | 0.9 | 0.9 | 0.1 |
| México (11097516) | 91.2 | 3.8 | 1.5 | 1.8 | 0.9 |
| CDMX (7738307) | 90.4 | 3.5 | 1.4 | 2.9 | 1.1 |
| **Nation's (84794454)** | **88** | **6.2** | **2** | **3.5** | **0.4** |
| Nvo León (3392025) | 87.9 | 6.2 | 2 | 2.8 | 0.1 |
| Sonora (1956617) | 87.8 | 4.9 | 1.8 | 4.3 | 0.1 |
| Coahuila (2018053) | 86.4 | 6.8 | 1.8 | 3.8 | 0.1 |
| Oaxaca (3019103) | 84.8 | 7.7 | 2.3 | 4 | 0.3 |
| Chihuahua (2621057) | 84.6 | 7.1 | 2 | 5.1 | 0.1 |
| Tamaulipas (2427309) | 82.9 | 8.6 | 2.3 | 4.9 | 0.3 |
| Veracruz (6118108) | 82.9 | 6.9 | 3.3 | 5.9 | 0.2 |
| Baja Calif (2010869) | 81.4 | 7.9 | 2.7 | 6.1 | 0.3 |
| Tabasco (1664366) | 70.4 | 13.6 | 5 | 10 | 0.2 |
| Chiapas (3288963) | 63.8 | 13.9 | 8 | 13.1 | 0 |

Source: Author's own creation on the basis of *La diversidad religiosa en México. XII Censo general de población y vivienda.* INEGI. México, 2005.

[a] Total population of five years and more appear in brackets

[b] Comprises Historical Protestant churches (Presbyterian, Baptist, Methodist, of the Nazarene, Mennonite, and other), and Evangelical churches (Evangelical and Pentecostal)

[c] Comprises Jehovah's Witnesses, Seventh-day Adventists and Mormons (The Church of Jesus Christ of Latter-day Saints)

[d] Comprises Buddhism, Islam, Judaism, Spiritualism, of native origin, and other

| | | Religious Resonance in Selected States, 2010. | | | |
|---|---|---|---|---|---|
| States[a] | % Catholic | % Protestant and Evangelical[b] | % biblical non-Evangelical[c] | % dissonant | % other[d] |
| Guanajuato (5486372) | 93.8 | 2.6 | 0.9 | 1.4 | 0.04 |
| Jalisco (7350682) | 92 | 3.2 | 1 | 1.7 | 0.3 |
| México (15175862) | 85.4 | 5.6 | 1.6 | 3.2 | 0.3 |
| **Nation's (112336538)** | **82.7** | **7.5** | **2.3** | **4.7** | **0.1** |
| CDMX (8851080) | 82.5 | 5.4 | 1.4 | 5.5 | 0.5 |
| Nvo León (4653458) | 82.4 | 8.2 | 2 | 4.1 | 0.05 |
| Sonora (2662480) | 82.3 | 7.7 | 2 | 6.5 | 0.06 |
| Oaxaca (3801962) | 80.6 | 10.5 | 2.7 | 4.5 | 0.1 |
| Coahuila (2748391) | 80.4 | 10 | 1.9 | 5.5 | 0.04 |
| Veracruz (7643194) | 78.7 | 9.2 | 3.3 | 6.5 | 0.08 |
| Chihuahua (3406465) | 76.4 | 9.5 | 2 | 7.4 | 0.03 |
| Tamaulipas (3268554) | 73 | 12.2 | 2.5 | 6.7 | 0.03 |
| Baja Calif (3155070) | 72 | 11.9 | 3.1 | 10 | 0.1 |
| Tabasco (2238603) | 64.5 | 18.4 | 5.6 | 9.5 | 0.04 |
| Chiapas (4796580) | 58.3 | 19.2 | 8.2 | 12.2 | 0.06 |

Source: Author's own creation on the basis of *Panorama de las religiones en México 2010*. INEG. México, 2011.

[a] Total population appear in brackets

[b] Comprises Historical Protestant churches (Anabaptist/Mennonite, Baptist, of the Nazarene, Methodist, Presbyterian, and other), and Evangelical churches (Evangelical and Pentecostal)

[c] Comprises Jehovah's Witnesses, Seventh-day Adventists and Mormons (The Church of Jesus Christ of Latter-day Saints)

[d] Comprises churches of Eastern origin, Judaism, Islam, of ethnic roots, Spiritualism, and other

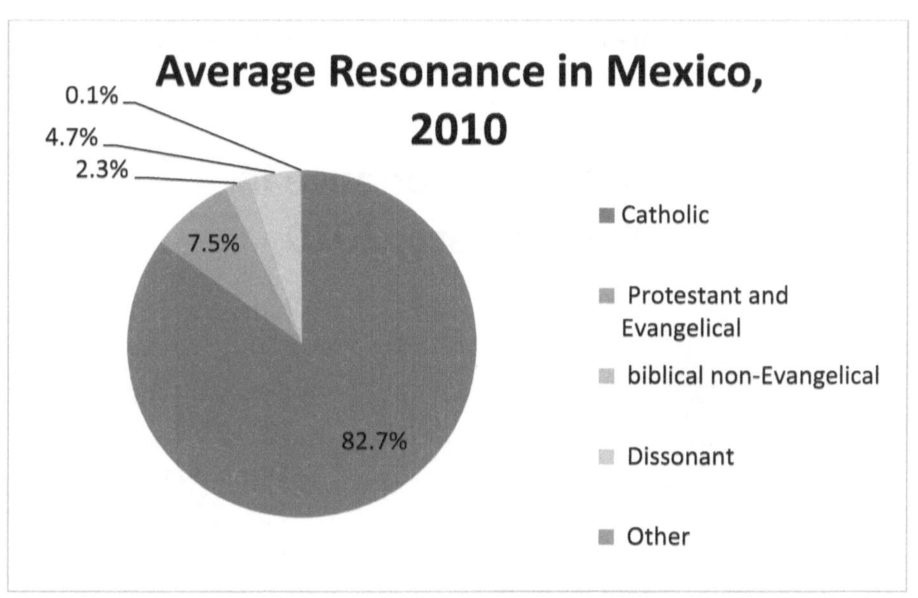



Is there any evidence of a regional distribution of the religious resonance in Mexico? The answer is the affirmative. The Catholic resonance clusters in the central-western part of the country, while the Protestant and Evangelical resonance cluster in the south-southeastern part of the territory (INEGI 2005, 27, 35, 43; De la Torre and Gutiérrez Z. 2007, 37). By 2000, the northern states which border with the US (Baja California, Sonora, Chihuahua, Coahuila, Nuevo Leon and Tamaulipas) show a Catholic resonance below the national figure; by 2010 the gap deepens and Baja California, the least Catholic of all, is ten percent below Mexico's Catholic resonance. It is true that the Protestant and Evangelical resonance of these states is above the national figure –the exception is Sonora in 2000–, though the data never go beyond the five percent mark. Finally, with the exception of the state of

25

Nuevo Leon, all states that border with the US clearly show a percentage of religious dissonance above the national figure.

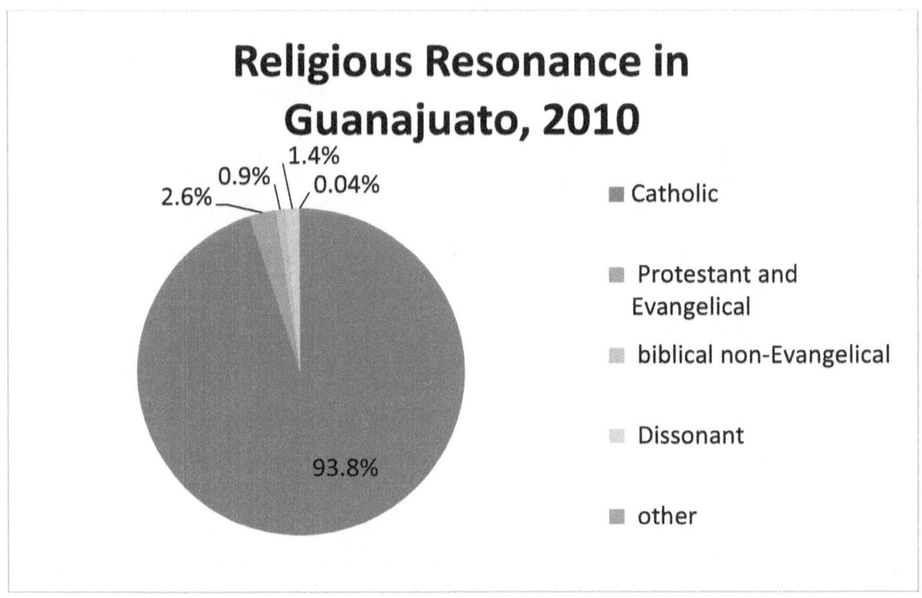



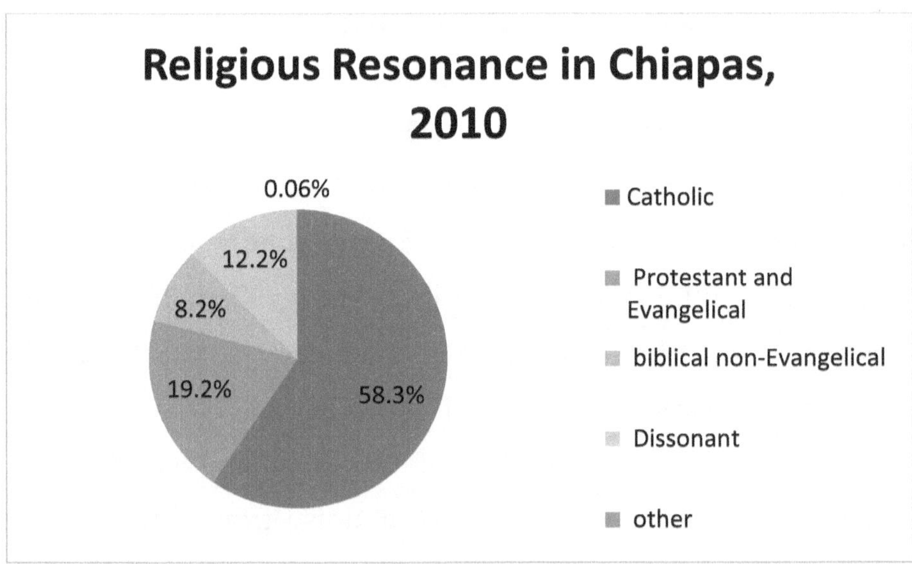

Mexico City (CDMX) stands out with an extreme dynamism which coincides with the outlined national tendencies above: besides experiencing the increase of the Protestant and Evangelical resonance (3.5 to 5.4%), in the last decade Catholicism lost almost eight percentage points resonance in Mexico City (90.4 to 82.5%) –under the national average by 2010–, and dissonant population increased considerably (2.9 to 5.5%, above the national average).

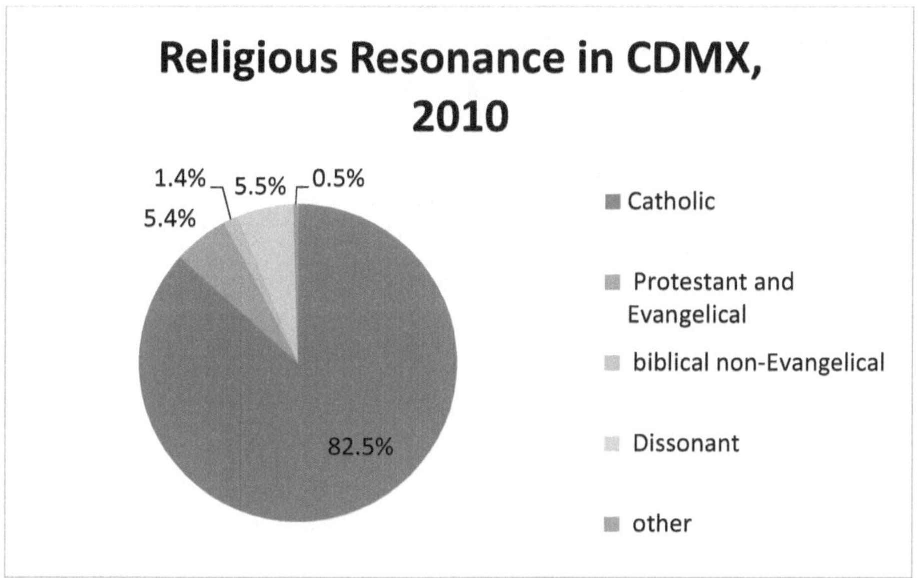


This is the moment to distinguish among the different Protestantisms in Mexico. Table 3 and its graphs establish the relative importance of the Protestant resonance in Mexico. Protestantism in Mexico, in terms of numbers, is primarily Evangelical and Pentecostal resonance –in that order–, and only then Historical Protestant resonance (traditional Protestant denominations).

| | Table 3. Protestant Resonance in Chosen States, 2010.[a] | | | | |
|---|---|---|---|---|---|
| States | % Historical Protestant (Nation's = 820744) | States | % Evangelical (Nation's=5595116) | States | % Pentecostal[b] (Nation's = 1970347) |
| Chiapas (287945) | 35.1 | Chiapas (225935) | 4 | Chiapas (407477) | 20.7 |
| Veracruz (25212) | 3.1 | Veracruz (325535) | 5.8 | Veracruz (351896) | 17.9 |
| Oaxaca (32696) | 4 | Oaxaca (192506) | 3.4 | Oaxaca (174266) | 8.8 |
| Tabasco (104652) | 12.7 | Tabasco (164284) | 2.9 | Tabasco (142341) | 7.2 |
| Tamps (26967) | 3.3 | Tamps (286498) | 5.1 | Tamps (84161) | 4.3 |
| Baja Calif (14956) | 1.8 | Baja Calif (297824) | 5.3 | Baja Calif (65057) | 3.3 |
| México (22641) | 2.8 | México (766978) | 13.7 | México (62046) | 3.1 |
| Nvo León (28095) | 3.4 | Nvo León (305855) | 5.5 | Nvo León (48923) | 2.5 |
| Coahuila (21283) | 2.6 | Coahuila (220551) | 3.9 | Coahuila (34304) | 1.7 |
| Sonora (8936) | 1.1 | Sonora (163587) | 2.9 | Sonora (31338) | 1.6 |
| CDMX (18062) | 2.2 | CDMX (437889) | 7.8 | CDMX (20291) | 1 |
| Chih (15830) | 1.9 | Chih (286981) | 5.1 | Chih (20425) | 1 |

Source: Author's own creation on the basis of *Panorama de las religiones en México 2010*. INEG. México, 2011.

[a] The total population for different Protestant denominations appears in brackets

[b] Comprises Pentecostal and neo-Pentecostal churches, and churches with Pentecostal roots (Iglesia del dios vivo, columna y apoyo de la verdad, la luz del mundo)

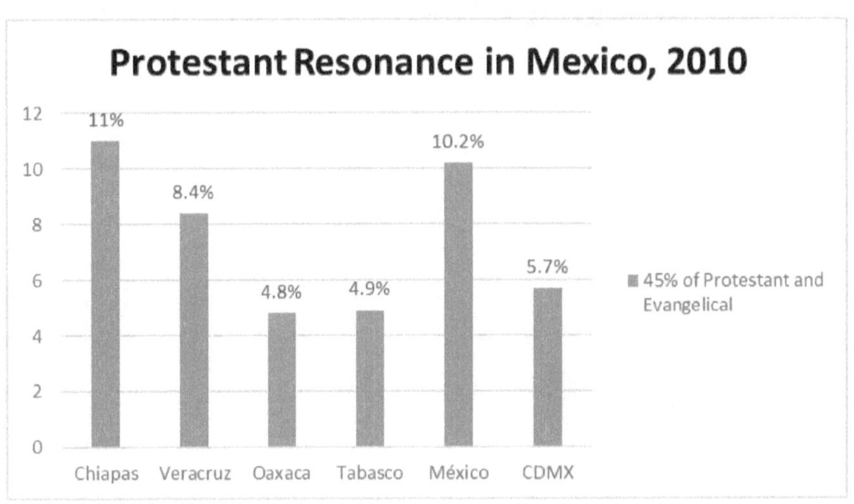


The "Evangelical", "Christian" or "Pentecostal" churches do not refer to the same denomination, "but to a constellation of groups who identify themselves in terms of doctrine, but do not formally belong to one same organization" (INEGI 2005, 18ff). What identifies them is a doctrinal affinity with Historical Protestantism, and an extreme organizational fragmentation that borders on autarchy. The distinction between Evangelicals and Pentecostals is ambiguous (Gutiérrez Z. and De la Torre 2007, 93) since they both name themselves after "Evangelicals", in particular to make evident their sense of unity against the Catholic "image worshippers".[13] It is also true that the word "Pentecostal" may not be present in many Pentecostal churches' official names.

---

[13] The amplitude of the term "Evangelical", allows Garma (2007, 80) to assert that Pentecostal associations represent "the non-Catholic religious associations with the greatest number of faithful in the country".

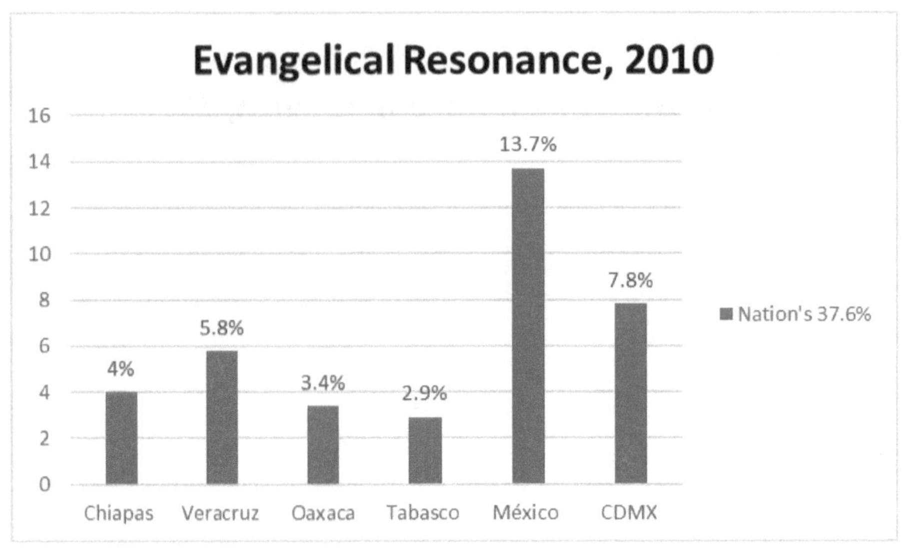



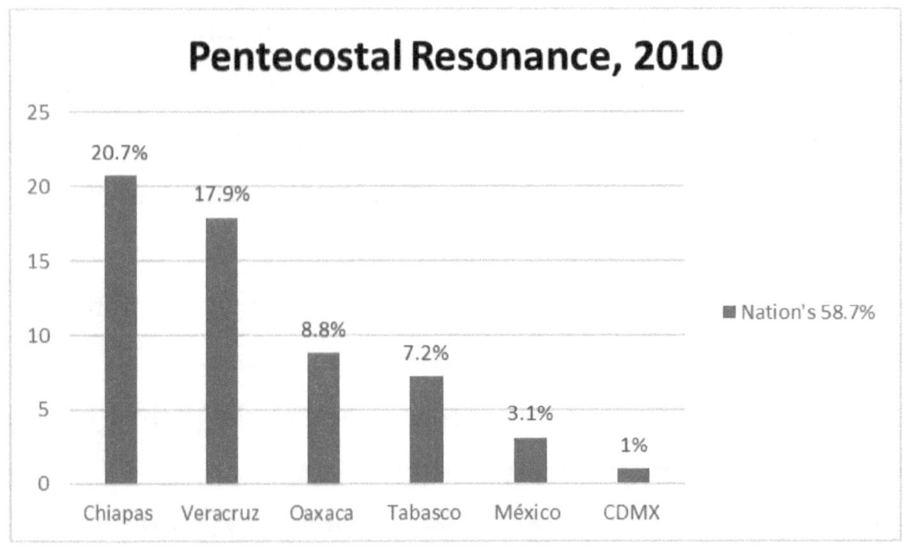



Historical Protestantism is the branch of Christianity that groups "the churches close to the Protestant Reformation of the sixteenth century, which caused the separation of the Catholic Church from the Reformed churches" (INEGI 2005, 16ff). These Protestant societies have been present in Mexico since the nineteenth century (Gutiérrez Z. 2007, 50). INEGI's grouping of Protestant denominations –there are Historical and Evangelical Protestants, and within the Evangelical some that are called Pentecostals or Pentecosteses– is strongly influenced by the studies of Jean Pierre Bastian (2006; 1992) on Mexican Protestantism.

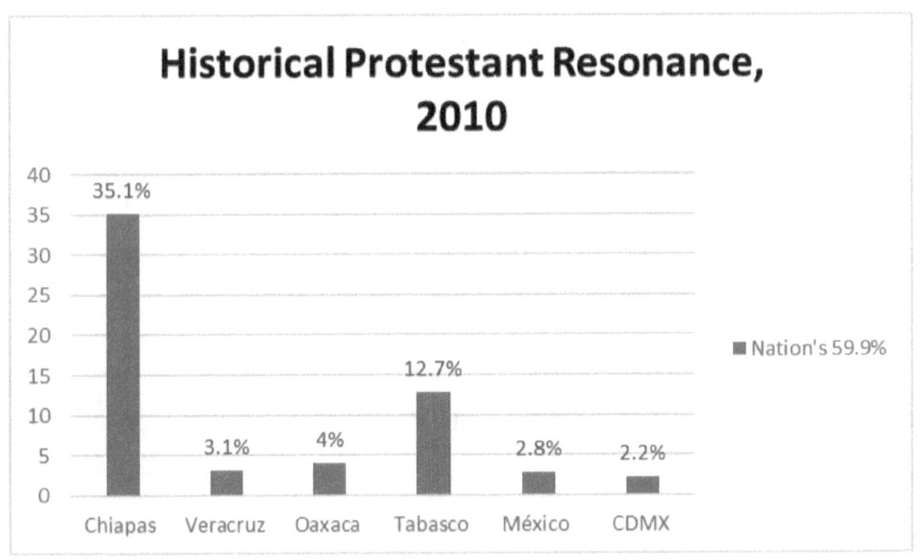


Table 3 provides information on the resonance of specifically Protestant communications in Mexico. Columns show the importance of selected states in the distribution of the Mexican Protestantisms: Historical, Evangelical and Pentecostal. It could be noted, for example, that Chiapas and Tabasco concentrate 47.8% of the Historical Protestant resonance in Mexico (mostly of the Presbyterian kind). In Oaxaca, with 4% of the Historical Protestant resonance in the country, the Baptist branch is predominant (INEGI 2005, 16). The state of Mexico, the one with

31

the greatest Evangelical resonance, concentrates 13.7% of the country's Evangelicals (INEGI 2005, 18). The northern states which border with the US concentrate more than one fourth of Mexico's Evangelical resonance (27.8%), which is not to be overemphasized since these states make up only 23.4% of Mexico's Protestant and Evangelical resonance. Tamaulipas and Baja California show a remarkable Pentecostal resonance yet still under the levels of Chiapas, Veracruz, Oaxaca and Tabasco.

Finally, the three states with the greatest number of Pentecostals (Chiapas, Veracruz and Oaxaca) concentrate almost half (more than 47%) of the Mexican Pentecostal resonance.[14] Chiapas alone concentrates more than one third of Mexico's Historical Protestants (35.1%), and is the state with the least Catholic resonance (58.3%), and consequently, the state in Mexico with the greatest plain Protestant resonance (11%). According to these figures the "Protestantization" of the south-southeast of Mexico means "Pentecostalization" clearly in the cases of Chiapas, Veracruz and Oaxaca. Nationwide, the Protestantization is best represented by Chiapas, which has the least Catholic resonance in Mexico. The Protestantization of Mexico means the primacy of

---

[14] Coincidently, these three states in a different order of importance –Chiapas, Oaxaca and Veracruz–, concentrate almost all the municipalities in the country where the Catholic resonance is a minority (De la Torre and Janssen 2007, 124), inhabited mainly by indigenous populations (Garma and Hernández 2007, 203).

Evangelical resonance, and only then the increasing importance of the Pentecostal resonance.[15]

## 2.2 Ministers of Cult and Religious Associations.

There are more Protestant and Evangelical ministers of cult registered with the Mexican governmental authority –Dirección General de Asociaciones Religiosas de la Secretaría de Gobernación– than registered Catholic priests, which is out of tune with the figures of Catholic resonance in the country. This is clearly shown in Table 4. In 2014, with at least 80% of Catholic resonance in Mexico, Catholic registered priests were not even one fourth of the total (23.1%). In contrast, around 10% of Protestant and Evangelical resonance summed up almost half of the registered ministers of cult in Mexico (48.3%).

[15] More emphatically than Garma does (refer to fn. 13), Hernández (2007) contends that Pentecostals exceed the number of Evangelicals in Mexico, though this assertion does not stand the official data shown above in Table 3. Percentages given by him: 64% of Pentecostal, 25% of Evangelical, and 11% of Historical Protestant resonance (against the 23%, 67%, and 10% official figures, respectively).

Table 4. Registered Ministers of Cult: 2007, 2014.

| Nation's total | % Catholic | % Protestant and Evangelical | % biblical non-Evangelical[a] | % other[b] |
|---|---|---|---|---|
| | | | | |
| 2007=60392[c] | 32.3 | 57.4 | 9.7 | 0.4 |
| 2014=88219[d] | 23.1 | 48.3 | 28.3 | 0.3 |
| | | | | |

Sources: Author's own creation with data taken as indicated.
[a] Comprises Jehovah's Witnesses, Seventh-day Adventists and Mormons
[b] Comprises Eastern (Hindu, Buddhist, Krishnas), Jew, Orthodox Christian, Islamic, and those who belong to new religious expressions
[c] Data taken from *Ministros registrados por credo religioso*. www.asociacionesreligiosas.gob.mx. September 3, 2007.
[d] Data taken from *Ministros de culto por tradición* al 2 de mayo de 2014. www.asociacionesreligiosas.gob.mx/es/AsociacionesReligiosas/Numeralia. May 20, 2014.

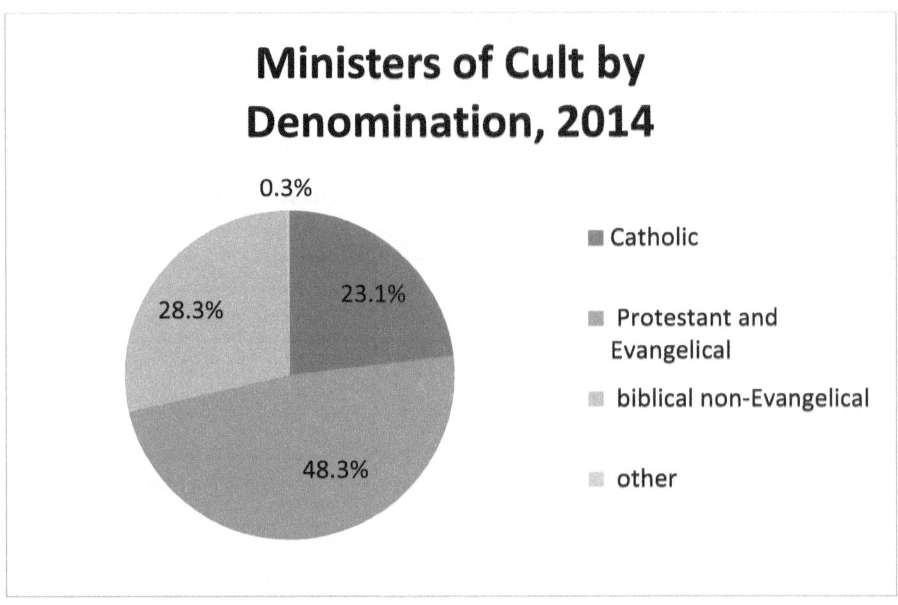


The requirements imposed on candidates to ministers of cult by different churches could explain in some way this disproportion. For example, Catholic priesthood requires at least an equivalent to a Bachelor of Arts degree, though this could as well be explained by the simple inflation of the Catholic resonance –for representing the traditional religion of contemporary Mexico, the religion imposed since colonial times– and by the vocational crisis experienced in Catholicism in general. In any case, the population attended by registered cult ministers is shocking: 4 560 Catholic faithful attended per priest against only 197 Protestants attended per pastor, as is shown in Table 5 (data for 2014).

Table 5. Faithful Attended per Minister of Cult: 2007, 2014.

| Year | Catholic | Protestant and Evangelical | Biblical non-Evangelical | other |
|------|----------|----------------------------|--------------------------|-------|
| **2007** | 4764 | 242 | 433 | 714 |
| **2014** | 4560 | 197 | 102 | 65 |

Sources: Own creation on the basis of Table 4 and *Panorama de las religiones en México 2010*. INEG. México, 2011.

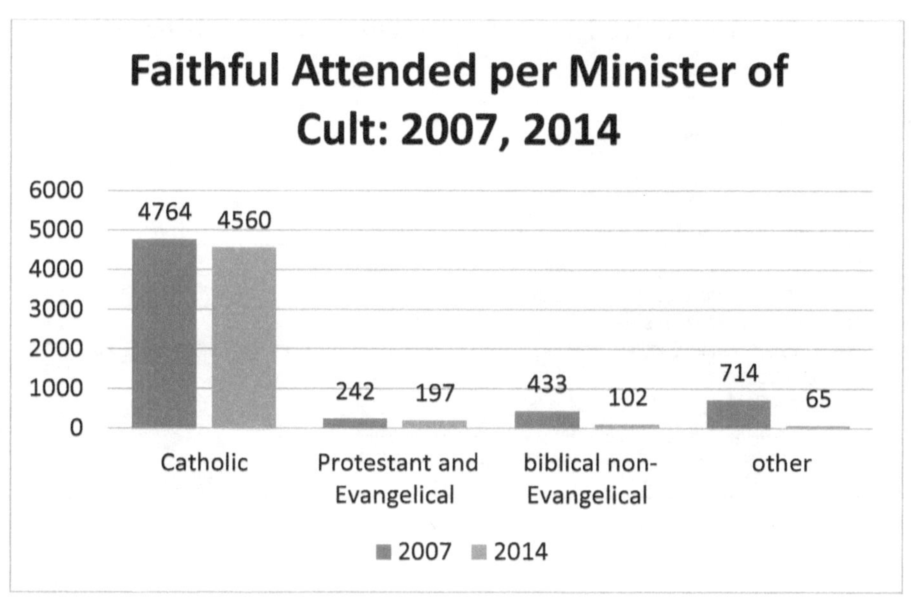

Table 6 presents data for registered religious associations for 1998 and 2014. Here again the figures are disproportionate with the Catholic religious resonance. For example, in 2014, around 80% of Mexicans who profess Catholicism groups in only 41% of the registered associations in the country (3 223 associations), which allows for stacking up 28 831 faithful per Catholic association. As is the case with population attended per minister of cult one can presuppose an inflated Catholic resonance or the prominent flexibility of the Catholic commitment –compatible with the increasing secularization of world society–, only comparable with today's commitment of soccer fans to their colors. The extreme centralization of the Catholic organization, pyramidal in type, may as well play a part in this situation.

Table 6. Registered Religious Associations: 1998, 2014.

| Nation's total | % Catholic | % Protestant and Evangelical | % biblical non-Evangelical[a] | % other[b] |
|---|---|---|---|---|
| | | | | |
| 1998=5266[c] | 19 | 48.4 | n.s. | 32.6[d] |
| 2014=7976[e] | 40.9 | 58.1 | 0.2 | 0.8 |

Sources: Own creation with data taken as indicated.
[a] Comprises Jehovah's Witnesses, Seventh-day Adventists and Mormons
[b] Comprises Eastern (Hindu, Buddhist, Krishnas), Jew, Orthodox Christian, Islamic, and those which belong to new religious expressions
[c] Data taken from Garma (1999,138)
[d] Comprises biblical non-Evangelical, for whose there is not information available
[e] Data taken from *Asociaciones religiosas por tradición* al 2 de mayo de 2014. www.asociacionesreligiosas.gob.mx/es/AsociacionesReligiosas/Numeralia. May 20, 2014.

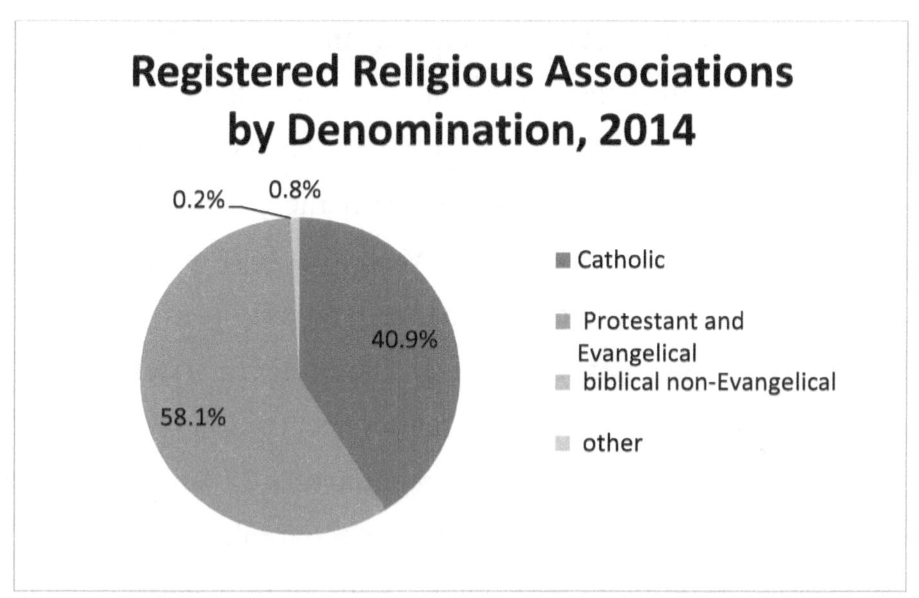



## 2.3 Conclusion

Even though in Mexico Catholic resonance is of 82.7%, there exist
no less than 15 denominations different from Catholicism. The
non-Catholic resonance reaches almost 10% of the total
population, and religious dissonance is close to 5% of the
inhabitants. Protestant and Evangelical communications are the
most important competitors of the Catholic communications. The
religious resonance has a clear regional expression: while the
Catholic resonance concentrates in the central-western states,
Protestant and Evangelical communications concentrate in the
south-southeast of Mexico.

Chiapas, Mexico and Veracruz are the states with the greatest
number of Protestants in Mexico. The state of Mexico has the

greatest Evangelical resonance (13.7%), while Chiapas is the least Catholic of the country (58.3%), and has the greatest Historical Protestant and Pentecostal resonance (35.1%, of the Presbyterian type, and 20.7%, respectively) in Mexico. The states of Chiapas, Veracruz and Oaxaca concentrate together the greatest Pentecostal resonance. The Protestantization of Mexico is first of all predominance of Evangelical resonance, and only then, increasing importance of Pentecostal resonance. The northern states which border with the US show an important concentration of Evangelical resonance that reaches the nation's 27.8%. It could be said that as one goes further north in the geography, leaving behind territories with a high concentration of indigenous populations, Protestantism acquires a more rational hue and less a magical and patriarchal one.

Contrary to the data of religious resonance in Mexico, 48.3% of the nation's registered ministers of cult belong to Protestant and Evangelical denominations, against only 23.1% of Catholic priests. The relationship of faithful to ministers of cult is above 4 500 to 1 for Catholicism, and of only 127 to 1 for Protestant and Evangelical denominations. Something quite similar happens for registered religious associations, where less than half of them belong to Catholicism (40.9%), which pretend to look after no less than 80% of Mexico's population. These data give place to a confident prediction of an inflated Catholic resonance in Mexico otherwise called nominal Catholicism.

# 3. Shamanistic Trance, Gift of Tongues or Kriya?[16]

## Chapter Abstract

This chapter emphasizes that glossolalia/ kriya phenomena are different ways of communicating religious meanings depending on particular ritual contexts –as such, glossolalia/ kriya phenomena are religiously meaningless, unless they are said to be "gifted by the Holy Spirit" or, else, to represent "an awakening of kundalini"–. Literally speaking: from the point of view adopted in this paper, the way of phrasing glossolalia/ kriya phenomena points to a particular religious framing (the phrasing is the framing). The bridging of the gap between cultures was made possible, historically speaking, through a particular colonial process (the British Raj in India), and Protestant missionary work (The Mukti Mission in Pune, India) which in turn gave way to structural change with impact in the lives of whole peoples. Hybrid communicational processes became a feasible event through the life of Pandita Ramabai (1858-1922).

Once we have seen Mexican religious differentiation and its characteristic features, we can rehearse a history of the emergence of world Pentecostalism. As will be seen throughout the chapter, this exercise owes much to the theoretical approach used. This is so because the chapter will provide a cross-observation –the concept that designates it is *hetero-reference*– of the emergence of modern Pentecostalism as it is offered by social science and, in particular, as it is offered by the social systems program (theory) of social science. Cross-observations (comparisons) between social systems and religions (religious programs), as we will see in

---

[16] An independent article of this chapter was published by the Chilean Universidad Arturo Prat (Ornelas 2018a).

what follows, are consubstantial to this sociological theory of communication.[17]

As the reader may already know, glossolalia or speaking-in-tongues is the spontaneous, involuntary capacity to generate mumbling or foreign speech which usually happens in the context of ritual practices and which is supposed –though not necessarily– to convey a meaning.[18] In what follows, the terms glossolalia and xenoglossia will be used interchangeably, as does the literature on this subject. The slight difference in both terms is that glossolalia, unlike xenoglossia, is not immediately recognizable as a foreign language (German, French or Japanese). In twentieth century Christianity, glossolalia acquired importance with the appearance of Evangelical revival groups –so called Pentecostals– who claimed that glossolalia was not only an ecstatic religiously induced state, but could as well signal having "been touched by the Holy Spirit".

On the other hand, kriya is a spontaneous body motion, mumbling or speech in an unknown language which in traditional religious Hindu literature is supposed to signal the "awakening" of

---

[17] As can be noted, science as such, within the theory of social systems, ceases to observe society from an external and privileged point of view, as if it were done from an ivory tower. What the theory affirms for religious communication, also affirms it for scientific communication itself. Is not this a more than just treatment, on the part of science, of the relations established by science and religion?

[18] Kavan (2004, 171) defines glossolalia as "a verbal utterance in a religious context, which is not in the speaker's own language".

kundalini[19] or the spiritual energy that coils dormant at the base of the spine. The words kriya and karma share the same Sanskrit root (*kri*, meaning "to do"). Kriya would mean an action, deed or effort. Krishna lists, among the possible paths to spiritual attainment, that of karma yoga in the known fragment of the *Mahabharata*, the Bhagavad Gita or Song of the Lord.

The study of glossolalia has been given lately much attention due to the fact that Pentecostalism represents one of the most dynamic world religious communication systems, and because speaking-in-tongues is considered by most Pentecostal churches as evidence of being gifted by the Holy Spirit. Moreover, a classical study has shown that glossolalia includes a wide range of manifestations – from uttering simple sounds to speaking foreign languages–, and that glossolalia phenomena may be found in different religious and cultural settings.

Here we emphasize that glossolalia/ kriya phenomena are different ways of communicating religious meanings depending on particular ritual contexts –as such, glossolalia/ kriya phenomena are religiously meaningless, *unless they are said* to be "gifted by the Holy Spirit" or, else, to represent "an awakening of kundalini"–.[20] What matters here is that the bridging of the gap

---

[19] An introductory treatise on kundalini and its workings could be found in Kripananda (1995); a  comprehensive treatise by a British Orientalist could be found in Avalon (1950).

[20] A sociological theory of religious communication would regard glossolalia/ kriya phenomena as symbiotic symbols, that is, the body's capacity to interfere with religious

between cultures was made possible, historically speaking,
through a particular colonial process (the British Raj in India), and
Anglican missionary work (The Mukti Mission in Pune, India)
which in turn gave way to structural change with impact in the
lives of whole peoples. We will be interested in showing how
hybrid communicational processes became a feasible event
through the life of Pandita Ramabai (1858-1922).

## 3.1 The Multiple Religious Programming of One Same Event

There has been many accounts of non-Christian occurrences of
glossolalia, such as the classical survey conducted by May (1956)
with spiritualism, shamanistic practices and religions worldwide.
May showed how glossolalia[21] phenomena fit a whole range of
trance-like and shamanistic practices. For example, Siberian
shamans imitate "the cries and sounds of animals, birds, and
natural phenomena as a sign that he can transform himself at will
into a nonhuman embodiment and circulate freely among the three
cosmic zones: hell, earth, and heaven" (May 1956, 81).

In the Andean region, the *curanderos* (healers) mumble prayers as
they ingest drugs and suck the area of the patient's affliction.

---

communication (Luhmann 2007a, 295ff; 2009, 153ff). Of course, there are multiple ways
in which glossolalia/ kriya phenomena may be religiously communicated; in what
follows we will see examples of these.

[21] This survey defines glossolalia as "ecstatic vocalization in the form of incoherent
sounds and foreign words" or/and as "verboauditive, vocal, verbovisual, and graphic
automatisms" (May 1956, 75-76).

Glossolalia is also found among the Niue shamans of south Polynesia, whereas people allegedly possessed by demons show a similar behavior in China. A native priest bows and mumbles before the idols at a Zapotecan (Mexican) funeral ceremony.

Speaking inadvertently in foreign tongues (*xenoglossia*) is practiced among Eskimos in Alaska, natives in Guyana, and is also practiced in African religions as well as in dervish rites in Iraq. Relating to India, May tells us about how a Todas entranced priest was able to speak in Malayalam at a funeral but unable to do it in a normal conscious state (May 1956, 84). Buddhism has an explanation of glossolalia phenomena based in the doctrine of the transmigration of souls (he/she who experiences xenoglossia was born in a past life in the country where that particular tongue is spoken).

Moreover, a study by Kavan (2004) in New Zealand takes for granted that Pentecostals and yoga practitioners experience glossolalia. At times, glossolalia may be produced under "altered states of consciousness". The transmission of energy by a spiritual leader to yoga practitioners (called *shaktipat*) is similar to what Pentecostals experience as the baptism of the Spirit, which in most cases unleashes glossolalia experiences (Kavan 2004, 174).

Kavan also reports that yoga practitioners "occasionally experienced glossolalia as a *kriya* (manifestation) of the purificatory process and whose spiritual experiences appeared to be closer to those of early Pentecostals" (Kavan 2004, 171-172). She concludes that Pentecostals and charismatics experience glossolalia most of the times in a normal state of consciousness, since this is expected from them, that is, glossolalia is regarded as an extraordinary though a necessary signal of the intervention of the Spirit: "The routinization of glossolalia and decline in spiritual experience appear to be linked" (Kavan 2004, 178). Thus, glossolalia among Christian New Zealanders is more a self-inflicted, simulated state than a real trance-like experience.

Given the evidence provided by social anthropology and religious studies, it could be said with certainty that glossolalia phenomena have been present in a great variety of cultures since time immemorial. Also, it should be noted that glossolalia, even within Christianity, is a much more complex phenomenon than mere speaking-in-tongues, as an early account stated: "This speaking in tongues is but one of a series of such phenomena as 'tongues of fire', 'rushing of a mighty wind', 'interpretation of tongues', jerking, writhing, and falling to the ground, which are occurring in connection with a world-wide religious revival" (Henke 1909, 193).

It is not our concern here to claim where glossolalia first originated, neither to support the idea that it first originated in a particular cultural setting and from there it passed into another.[22]

---

[22] None of these would serve the purpose of picturing sociocultural complexity. Here we favor the concept of "equifinality", by which is meant that different systemic states may

We are only interested in providing a feasible historical account of a true contact between cultures. This contact, as we have tried to explain elsewhere (Ornelas 2018b), involves communicational complex events with structural couplings present in the (religious) communicational, psychic and physical/organic levels, and persons with first and last name, in our present case, Pandita Ramabai.

3.2 The Mukti[23] Mission and its Importance to the Pentecostal Revival.

The first known accounts of Pentecostal revivals in the American continent seems to be either that of Charles Parham in Topeka, Kansas in 1900, or that of William J. Saymour of the Azusa Street Mission in Los Angeles, California in 1906 (Robeck Jr., 2014; Bastian, 2006). Robeck Jr. notes that both were actually directly connected, as Parham visited Saymour in LA, though they parted from each other because they did not get along. These were followed

---

produce one same result, the Pentecostal revival. The equifinality concept indicates the possibility of a *worldwide* simultaneous emergence of Pentecostal groups or, if you will, a *drift* established by Christian communication from the nineteenth century, without the phenomenon having *necessarily* to be explained by simple causal relations. The theory of social systems uses this concept to discuss the co-occurrence of evolutionary acquisitions such as agriculture, alphabetical writing, money or the printing press (Luhmann 2007a, 399ff). In any case, the concept fits a "cumulative model" of structural change as understood by Stichweh (2008), or a "hybrid" approach to culture as given by Burke (2010).

[23] Mukti is a Sanskrit word that Christians feel comfortable to translate as "salvation", though a more appropriate definition would be that of "liberation or release" from samsara, the wheel of birth, death and rebirth. It could be used as a synonym of moksha.

in 1909 by the Chilean Pentecostal revival led by May Louise and Willis Hoover, both Episcopalian Missionaries in Valparaiso.[24]

Garma and Leatham (2004, 146-147) credit a woman, Romana Valenzuela, with being the first person of introducing the Pentecostal cult into northwest Mexico. She had got in touch and converted to Evangelicalism through the Azusa Street Mission in 1912, and founded her own congregation in Villa Aldama, Chihuahua, in 1914, the Iglesia Apostólica de la Fe en Cristo Jesús. The Asambleas de Dios (Assemblies of God) followed Valenzuela's lead; they were introduced in Mexico in 1918.

As was the case with Pentecostalism in Africa, it seems that world Pentecostalism is linked to the previous ongoing existence of worldwide British colonial rule; an assertion that could very well be applied to the British Raj in India (1858-1947) and to Pune's Mukti Mission. Anderson expresses it quite simply:

> The existence of large and strong independent churches in southern Africa today has much to do with early Pentecostal missions. There are indications that Pentecostal missionaries tapped into a new phenomenon that was particularly strong in British colonial Africa, and especially in South Africa (Anderson 2014, 20).

The Mukti Mission, formally "non-denominational" (in reality: multidenominational), did nothing but reflect the relations

---

[24] In Orellana (2016) one can find a historical review of Chilean Pentecostalism through its two main churches: the Iglesia Metodista Pentecostal and the Iglesia Evangelica Pentecostal.

between the different Protestant missionary societies and Anglo-Saxon colonialism, as well as the tensions which derived from it. While in India Protestant evangelization was considered legitimate, in Latin America the legitimacy of such endeavor was questioned. The give-and-take was evident in the celebration of the World Missionary Conference of 1910 held in Edinburgh.

In the preparatory works for the conference, two clearly delineated positions were posed, represented by its two main organizers, John R. Mott of the United States, and J. H. Oldham of the United Kingdom. The difficulties arose with the insistence of North American Protestants to include Latin America within territories susceptible of being the object of Protestant missionary work, while the English, especially the Anglican Church, assumed that Protestant evangelization should leave untouched the territories that had already been evangelized by other Christian churches (Catholic, Eastern Christian or Orthodox). Finally, it was the English position which prevailed during its celebration (Piedra 2000, 113-161).

The change of direction in the Protestant evangelizing policy towards Latin America occurred until the Missionary Congress of Panama in 1916:

> The Congress of Panama of 1916 is considered as an event which marked a new era with respect to the presence and expansion of Protestantism in Latin America. It represented the end of a period when the presence of the Catholic Church led to the belief that, as a territory already occupied by Christianity, the work of Protestant missions was strange and illegitimate. On the other

hand, for the great missionary societies, the Congress signified the beginning of a conscious effort to extend its work throughout the Latin American continent, as never before. Protestant evangelization prior to this event depended heavily on the vision of small missionary societies, and in particular on the initiative of individuals. It was not until after 1916 that these efforts sought to be consolidated (Piedra 2000, 163).

The rearrangement in the gravitation of Anglo-Saxon colonialism in favor of the Americans had begun years ago with the victory of Mexican Liberals over Maximilian of Augsburg in 1867 (compare next chapter), and was strengthened by the triumph of the United States in the Hispanic-American War of 1898 –which brought them control over Cuba and the Philippines–, with the permanent control of the United States over the Panama Canal in 1903, and with the involvement of the United States in the First World War.

What seems clear is that American missionary societies had no qualms about working together with the colonial interests of their country. For example, for Samuel Inman of the Central American Mission (CAM):

> [...] the World War had helped to overcome the image of Latin America as a land of little value for investment, or as an area "composed of indigenous and illiterate people with little opportunity for trade". This idea, according to Inman, was contradicted by the wealth of Chilean nitrate, Argentina's wheat, Mexico's oil, Brazil's coffee, Cuba's sugar, Bolivia's tin, and Costa Rica's banana production. "Now... businessmen are convinced of how wrong that opinion is" (Piedra, 2000, 91).

This assessment is supported by Anderson (2014, 16-17):

> The various revival movements in Mukti, Los Angeles, and Valparaiso were all part of a series of events from which global

Pentecostalism emerged. Missionaries from these various revival movements went out into faith missions and independent missions, some joining Holiness and radical evangelical organizations like the Christian and Missionary Alliance and then became Pentecostal. The coming of the Spirit was linked to a belief that the last days had arrived and that the "full gospel" would be preached to all nations before the coming of the Lord. Considerations of religious pluralism, colonialism and cultural sensitivity were not on the agenda of those who rushed out to the nations with this revivalist message believing that they had been enabled to speak those languages they needed for the task.

Anderson also has noted the importance of Evangelical periodicals —the periodical of the Mukti Mission in Kedgaon: Mukti Prayer Bell (1906)— and missionary networks for the spread of world Pentecostalism. In his opinion:

> [...] the Welsh Revival (1904-5), the revivals in North-East and Central India (1905-7) and the Azusa Street revival in the USA (1906-9) were all part of a wider series of revivals that promoted Pentecostal beliefs and values throughout the world. In particular, a convincing case can be made to situate Pandita Ramabai's Mukti Revival in Kedgaon, near Pune in 1905-7, within the emerging Pentecostal movement; and Minnie Abrams, one of its leaders, was instrumental in passing on the news of this revival to inspire the emergence of Pentecostalism in the Methodist Church in Chile (Anderson 2014, 14).

The Mukti Mission in India paralleled the importance of the Azusa Street revival for world Pentecostalism. This observation of early modern Pentecostalism is in line with the idea of a multi-focal emergence of revival Evangelical Christian groups worldwide.[25] In

---

[25] For a recent account refer to Wilkinson (2015) whom, apart from bringing into question the alleged central role of the Azusa Street Mission, provides interesting Pentecostal distribution figures for various continents as well as its future trends.

fact, Pentecostal leaders in LA considered their revival as a consequence of the previous Mukti expansion:

> It is clear that the eyewitness and participant in the Azusa Street revival Frank Bartleman, its African American leader William Seymour, and the writers of its periodical The Apostolic Faith saw the Indian revival as a precedent to the one in which they were involved. It was seen as a prototypical, earlier Pentecostal revival that they thought had become "full-grown" in Los Angeles (Anderson 2014, 15).

1905-7, date provided by Anderson for the Mukti revival, seems to be a very late date. Historical sources point in contrast to 1896, immediately after the meeting of Ramabai with Rev. Gelson Gregson in the Lanouli Camp (compare what follows). An important starting point of modern Pentecostalism was the Keswick Convention that took place in 1875 in Cumbria, England. For a history of the early years of the Keswick Convention organized by an Anglican pastor, Thomas D. Harford-Battersby, and a Quaker, Robert Wilson, compare Harford (1907).

India's Mukti Mission also had a direct influence for the dissemination of Pentecostalism to Chile, as Minnie Abrams, former Methodist Episcopal missionary and Ramabai's assistant in the Mukti Mission, was acquainted with May Louise Hoover. Abrams sent Hoover accounts of the Mukti revival contained in her 1906 book *The Baptism of the Holy Ghost and Fire*,

> which in its second edition later that year included a discussion of the restoration of speaking in tongues.[26] This was the first written

---

[26] Though it should be noted that neither Abrams nor Ramabai considered speaking-in-tongues the unique and exclusive evidence of the baptism of the Spirit, as many

Pentecostal theology of Spirit baptism, and thirty thousand copies were circulated widely. As a result of this booklet and Abrams' subsequent correspondence with the Hoovers, the Methodist churches in Valparaiso and Santiago were stirred to expect and pray for a similar revival. The Pentecostal revival began in 1909, creating a schism in the Methodist Episcopal Church, and Willis Hoover became leader of the new Chilean Methodist Pentecostal Church consisting at first of those expelled from the Methodists (Anderson 2014, 16).

## 3.3 Pandita Ramabai: A Bridge between Cultures

Pandita Ramabai was born in the district of Mangalore, India, in 1858. Ramabai's father, Ananta Shastri, was a Brahmin reformer who thought that women could be taught to read and write in Sanskrit, against the traditional social prescriptions of Hinduism. Thus, Ramabai was indebted to her father's disposition for having learned Sanskrit as if it were her mother tongue. As a matter of fact, her parents made a living as Puranikas:

> Ever since I remember anything my father and mother were always travelling from one sacred place to another, staying in each place for some months, bathing in the sacred river or tank, visiting temples, worshipping household gods and the images of gods in the temples, and reading Puranas in temples or in some convenient place. The reading of the Puranas served a double purpose. The first and the foremost was that of getting rid of sin and of earning merit in order to obtain Moksha. The other purpose was to earn an honest living without begging. The readers of Puranas —Puranikas, as they are called— are the popular and public preachers of religion among the Hindus (Dyer 192?, 21).

In this way,

---

Pentecostal churches claim nowadays. Compare Merino (2012), who provides a good systematization of Pentecostal theology.

[...] the ponderous volumes which form the scriptures of Hinduism were all accessible to her, and she became familiar with their contents and doctrines. At twelve years of age she had committed to memory eighteen thousand verses from the Puranas. This religious learning forms the highest education of the Brahmin or priestly caste, to which Ramabai's family belonged (Dyer 1900, 10-11).

Apart from Kanarese (or Kannada) and Sanskrit, through her travelling Ramabai learned English, Marathi, Hindustani, and Bengali. The Hindu sacred literature had a clear stand on the place of women in society and of their possibilities for spiritual attainment:

> [...] there were two things on which all these books —the Dharma Shastras, the sacred epics, the Puranas and modern poets, the popular preachers of the present day, and orthodox high caste men, all were agreed— that women of high and low caste, as a class, were bad, very bad, worse than demons, as unholy as untruth and that they could not get Moksha as men... The extraordinary religious acts which help a woman to get into the way of getting Moksha are utter abandonment of her will to that of her husband. She is to worship him with whole-hearted devotion as the only god, to know and see no other pleasure in life except in the most degraded slavery to him. The woman has no right to study the Vedas and Vedanta, and without knowing them no one can know the Brahma; without knowing Brahma no one can get liberation, therefore no woman, as a woman, can get liberation (i.e., Moksha) (Dyer 192?, 26-27).

All this resulted in a deep religious dissatisfaction. In her own words:

> [...] while studying the *Dharma Shastras* they presented themselves to my mind with great force. My eyes were being gradually opened; I was waking up to my own hopeless condition as a woman, and it was becoming clearer and clearer to me that I had no place anywhere as far as religious consolation was concerned. I became quite dissatisfied with myself. I wanted

something more than the Shastras could give me, but I did not
know what it was that I wanted (Dyer 192?, 29).

This quote clearly shows the consciousness of a subordinated gender condition which is also common among Latin American indigenous women. Its feasibility is brought about either by migrations or by the intensification of contacts with mestizo society, which is to say: with the forever lost condition of communicational isolation.[27]

Ramabai and her family fell in economic hardship at the time of the 1876-77 famine in the Madras Presidency. Actually, the famine took the life of her parents and that of her older sister. Only her older brother survived it but, weakened, died later in Calcutta. "It was during these wanderings with her brother that Ramabai's faith in the Hindu religion was shaken, though until twenty years of age she worshipped the gods of brass and stone" (Dyer 1900, 17).

Here and elsewhere, Dyer's assertions, Ramabai's biographer and assistant during the first years of the Mukti Mission, show a cultural bias. This is to be considered an Anglican cross-cultural observation or *hetero-reference* (Luhmann 2007a, 697ff), although Ramabai might have approved such general stand in the matter. To explain her brother's ill health, Ramabai wrote:

My dear brother, a stalwart young fellow of twenty-one, spoilt his health and wasted his finely built body by fasting months and

---

[27] Compare Maier (2006) for Mexico's case, and Prieto et al. (2006) for Ecuador's.

months. But nothing came of all this futile effort to please the gods —the stone images remained as hard as ever, and never answered our prayers (Dyer 1900, 13).

Ramabai's fate changed for good in Calcutta, seat of British colonial power and first capital of the British Raj, where she lectured on the shastras (Hindu scriptures). There, she got in touch with Brahmins of the Brahmo Samaj, the Hindu reform movement... and with Christians, who presented her with a Sanskrit translation of the Bible (Dyer 192?, 25). She also met there her future husband, Bipin Bihari Medhavi, of the sudra caste, who died of cholera nineteen months after their civil marriage. Thus, Ramabai became a widow and was left alone with her little daughter, Manorama.

Ramabai made clear that, even though the Brahmo religion was much better than traditional Hinduism, it did not satisfy her at all:

> The Hindu religion held out no hope for me; the Brahmo religion
> was not a very definite one, for it is nothing but what a man
> makes for himself. He chooses and gathers whatever seems good
> to him from all religions known to him, and prepares a sort of
> religion for his own use. The Brahmo religion has no other
> foundation than man's own natural light, and the sense of right
> and wrong which he possesses in common with all mankind. It
> could not and did not satisfy me; still I liked and believed a good
> deal of it that was better than what the orthodox Hindu religion
> taught (Dyer 192?, 32).

During the 1880's Ramabai travelled to England (1883) and the United States (1886-88). In 1883, when baptized as a member of the Church of England, she would simply state that "I was hungry for something better than what the Hindu Shastras gave. I found it in the Christian's Bible and was satisfied" (Dyer 192?, 34). In 1887 Ramabai published *The High-Caste Hindu Woman* (Ramabai 1901), a book entirely devoted to report to the American reader the abuse and prejudices of orthodox Hinduism against women: how they were considered inferior to men, the marriage of women at a very young age, the spread practice of female infanticide, widow maltreatment, etc. Above all, this book contained an appeal to the American reader for financial support to the enterprise to which Ramabai would dedicate the rest of her lifetime.

Religious conversion in a Hindu context is hardly a smooth and straightforward decision. This is why it is appropriate to refer to the work of Meera Kosambi as an Indian contemporary source on Ramabai's case. In her opinion Ramabai's conversion into Christianity, and the response of the society of Maharashtra to it,

> need to be understood within a socio-temporal frame whose contours were shaped by British political, cultural, and racial supremacy which extended overt and covert patronage to Christianity, and which paradoxically nurtured the indigenous social reform movement with its nascent nationalistic overtones (Kosambi 1992, 61).

When Ramabai returned to India, she was most welcomed by the Hindu reformers:

> [...] the foremost welcome to India came to Ramabai from the Reform Hindus, known as the Brahmo Samaj. The leaders in this fraternity were largely the product of missionary education. They had been trained in missionary colleges. Their intellects had been convinced of the benefits of Christianity and of its social superiority to Hinduism; but they had rejected the Lord Jesus Christ. They no longer believed in the preposterous fables of their Hindu Shastras. They adopted many Christian customs and

imbibed a mixture of mild Hinduism and Unitarian doctrines; laid
down rules permitting the remarriage of widows, and raising the
age at which girls might remain unmarried. In short, they
established a sort of halfway-house to Christianity which turned
many a promising youth aside and deadened his conscience as
effectually as if he had remained in the toils of idolatry (Dyer
192?, 10).

The Brahmo Samaj could be considered as a reformation initiative
which brought Hinduism closer to Christianity.[28] One of its main
principles, the brotherhood of all human beings, was in stark
contrast with the caste system of Hinduism and became the
hallmark of the kind of Hinduism that was introduced to the West
by Swami Vivekananda (1863-1902) and some years later by
Paramahansa Yogananda (1893-1952).

If it is true that Buddhism and even Sikhism could be considered,
two millennia in between them, as early Hindu reform movements
which became new religions of their own accord, the Brahmo
Samaj remained inside Hinduism –Eliade and Couliano (1992,
177) refer to it as neo-Hinduism– and triggered the revaluation of
the spiritual legacy of Hinduism not just for India but *for world
society*. Along these lines one could pose the hypothesis that
through the Brahmo Samaj, Hinduism became a universal religion,
that is, it became a religion not attached anymore to caste, diet,

---

[28] A study of modern religious reformation movements in India may be found in
Farquhar (1915), in special the first two chapters. Besides giving the background of
British colonial presence (the East India Company) and of the arrival and development of
Anglican missionary work, this book provides biographical summaries of the Brahmo
Samaj founder and first leaders: Ram Mohan Ray, Debendra Nath Tagore, father of the
well-known poet and literature Nobel Prize winner, Rabindranath Tagore, and Keshab
Chandra Sen.

territory, and the like, available worldwide to everyone willing to adopt it.

Luhmann points out the possibility of an evolution of religious communication such as this one: "Among the most important results of religious evolution one must consider the emergence of *universal religions*... Universal religions are religions which offer their contents of faith to all human beings regardless ethnic, national or regional restrictions" (Luhmann 2007b, 238-239). This also assumes, of course, that British colonial rule turned out to be, at least indirectly, a major factor in this development.

Ramabai recalled her approach to Christianity: "I had failed to see the need of placing my implicit faith in Christ and His atonement in order to become a child of God by being born again of the Holy Spirit and justified by faith in the Son of God" (Dyer 192?, 36). And even provided a sort of theological reasoning on salvation:

> How very different the truth of God was from the false idea that I had entertained from my earliest childhood. That was, that I must have merit to earn present or future happiness, the pleasure of Svarga [heavenly worlds], or the utterly inconceivable lost condition of Moksha or liberation (Dyer 192?, 39).

In this sense, the Protestant doctrine of justification by faith alone fully counteracted the Hindu idea of an eternal search for merit – "good karma"– with the hope of attaining moksha someday.

Besides her conversion into Christianity, Ramabai founded the Ramabai Association with headquarters in Boston, USA (1887).

This association led to the establishment of the Mukti Mission (1889) for the relief of young widows in need, and guaranteed its financial support for a decade (the Sharada Sadan –"abode of wisdom"– initially in Bombay and later moved to Kedgaon, Pune).

By 1895, previous to the great famine of 1897, Ramabai experienced a spiritual yearning and finally was touched by the Holy Spirit:

> I read in the papers that Mr. Gelson Gregson  was to hold some special mission services in Bombay... In April at the Lanouli camp meeting I heard Mr. Gregson preach again. He preached as one who had received and was filled with the Holy Spirit and knew the deep things of God. I then opened my heart to a friend, and told her of my intense desire for the gift of the Holy Spirit; and we together sought a conversation with Mr. Gregson. I asked him many questions, which he satisfactorily answered in the words of Scripture. We prayed then that I might receive the Holy Spirit; but it was not until the evening of that day that I felt conscious of His presence in me. Since then I have received much blessing, and am ever grateful to God for showing me the way of this blessed life (Dyer 1900, 51).

Here, Ramabai's phrasing is already strongly resembling Keswick's new spirituality, or what might be called its distinctive charismatic theology (Brooke 1907, 75ff): a) first, sanctification by faith in Christ; b) then, the consecration by the Holy Spirit; and c) finally, the spread of the gospel to every corner of the planet (empowerment for mission).

According to Naselli (2008), what characterizes Keswick's initial spirituality is a sharp distinction between justification by faith alone, that is, the acceptance of Christ as the exclusive means of salvation, and the sanctification experienced in all areas of life as a consequence of this acceptance. Sometimes this sharp separation is referred to as *the crisis that follows conversion*. The statement also implies that this sanctification is not experienced by all the faithful, but only by those who have received the *baptism of the Spirit*, who in this way begin a progressive sanctification in their lives.

Reverend Gelson Gregson, former British army chaplain, took part of the Keswick Convention and was an active promoter of the charismatic spirituality which characterized it in its beginnings. (Battersby Harford 1907, 148).[29]

Apart from this direct contact with Keswick spirituality, Ramabai traveled again to the United States in 1898, when the support of the Ramabai Association to the Mukti Mission was about to end. Back in India, she had the opportunity to attend the Keswick Convention and to address it. In her own words:

> While there I received much blessing, and was greatly refreshed in my spirit. My heart was filled with joy to see nearly 4 000 people seeking and finding the deep things of God. At that time the Lord led me to ask those present to pray for an outpouring of the Holy Spirit on all Indian Christians. Five minutes were given me to speak, and I made the very best use of them. I requested God's people to pray that 100 000 men and 100 000 women from among the Indian Christians may be led to preach the Gospel to their country people (Dyer 192?, 66).

---

[29] More on the Keswick Convention in the next chapter.

Thus, the connection between the Keswick Convention and Pandita Ramabai's Mukti revival in India is out of question. Keswick spirituality followed the missionary model adopted by Hudson Taylor ("missions of faith") in the China Inland Mission in 1865. This missionary model was later disseminated by William Cameron Townsend and his Summer Institute of Linguistics/ Wycliffe Bible Translators (SIL-WBT), considered one of the most important American faith missions of the twentieth century (Aldridge 2012, 3ff; Hartch, 2006).

Ramabai, a widow herself, knew quite well the position of servitude and ignorance which women, in special widows, were expected to endure:

> [...] pupils began to come in, genuine Hindu widows with shaven heads, plain brick-red garments, and no jewellery. All the internal arrangements of the Home were designed to give perfect facility for Hindu customs to be carried out. Ramabai herself maintained her Hindu ways of living as regards food and clothing, though having become a Christian she was not permitted to eat with the Hindu pupils or even to enter their cookroom or touch their food lest she defile it! From the first there were two classes of pupils: the widows aforesaid; and the daughters of reformed Hindus, the Brahmas, who were less particular about keeping caste and who ate at the same table as Ramabai. The latter included a number of destitute young women whom Ramabai had rescued from moral danger, and for whose support she had made herself personally responsible and who were looked upon as her adopted daughters (Dyer 192?, 12).

Ramabai died in 1922. She witnessed the publication of the first edition of her translation of the New Testament into Marathi (1913), and also attested the sad and untimely death of her own daughter, Manorama, in 1921.

# 3.4 Conclusion

From all this three conclusions can be drawn. The first one is the equifinal character of sociocultural complexity, by which is meant that the new sociocultural selection –Pentecostal Christianity– is to be understood in the light of an ongoing evolutionary process which led to contemporary world society, and which triggered the adaptation of Hinduism so that it could be offered as a universal religion. Modern Pentecostalism emerges as a generalized cultural form of world society, whether this emergency is conceived through the concept of equifinality or, alternatively, as a planetary drift supported by dense networks of Anglo-Saxon missionaries (multidenominational) and in the world circulation of printed matter (missionary books and newspapers).

The second conclusion refers to the universal character of glossolalia/ kriya phenomena, but even more important than that, the actual possibility of referring to glossolalia/ kriya phenomena as symbiotic symbols, or in other words, as a multiple religious programming of one same event, depending on various ritual/ cultural settings: as a shamanistic trance, as the gift of tongues, or as the awakening of kundalini.

The last conclusion refers to the historical feasibility of structural change, which is related to the timing of various historical conditions that make possible the "bridging of cultures": colonial presence in India (the British Raj), an extreme economic hardship in the form of ever present famine in the late nineteenth century, an intense English educational and missionary activity (the Brahmo Samaj Hindu reform movement), and finally, the conversion of a learned Brahmin widow into a Christian (Pandita Ramabai and her Mukti Mission).

# 4. Evangelicals in Mexico City

Chapter Abstract

The central thesis of this final chapter is that Protestantism was imported from the United States at first by a minority of radical liberals (Benito Juarez and Sebastian Lerdo de Tejada), and later by the icon of Mexican revolutionary nationalism: Lazaro Cardenas del Rio. In both cases, the import was politically motivated and kept in step with the readjustment and consolidation of colonial powers. In time, the different variants of Protestantism led to inculturation and gave place to popular mestizo Evangelicalisms, patrimonial in kind rather than strictly modern. The characteristics of evangelical fundamentalism implanted in Mexico since the 1930s are consistent with the characteristics of Pentecostal and Neo-Pentecostal churches of Mexico City in which fieldwork was conducted.

The latest 2010 census data tell us that in Mexico the Catholic population accounts for 82.7% of the total population, while the evangelical population, including Para-Christian groups – Jehovah's Witnesses, Mormons and Seventh-Day Adventists–, add up 9.8%. Religiously dissonant population, that is, those who do not take hold of religious communication to guide their lives, reached 4.7% and, finally, 0.1% of the total population practice other religions.

Religious resonance in Mexico City is 82.5% Catholic, 6.8% evangelical and Para-Christian, 5.5% dissonant population, and 0.5% practice other religions. In short, in relation to the national average, in Mexico City there are fewer Catholics and evangelicals and Para-Christian groups, although there are more agnostics and many more practitioners of other religions.[30]

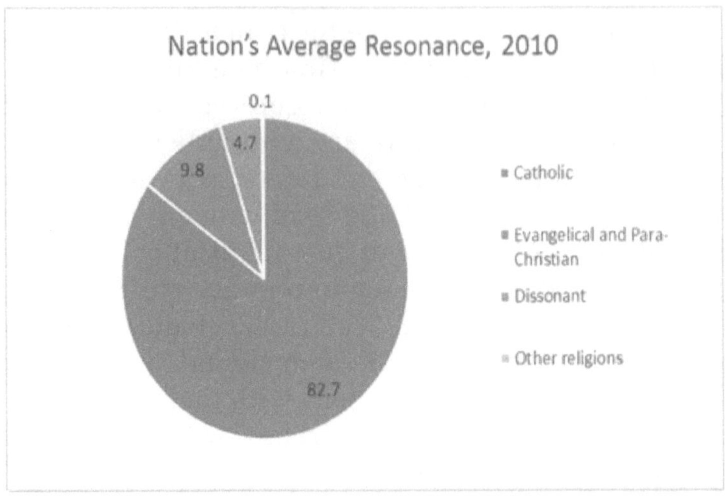


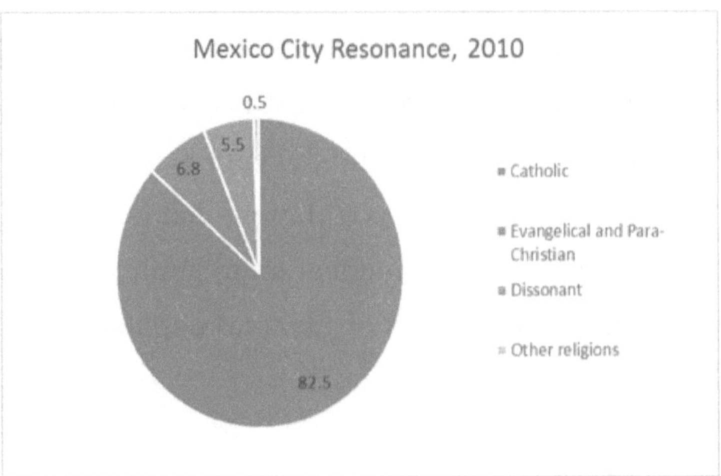


---

[30] Refer back to chapter 2. In this chapter we group the "Protestant and Evangelical" and "Biblical Non-Evangelical" census categories under the heading "Evangelical and Para-Christian".

This chapter attempts to provide a long-term assessment of the evolution of evangelical Christian communication in Mexico. Its central thesis is that Protestantism was imported from the United States at first by a minority of radical liberals (Benito Juarez and Sebastian Lerdo de Tejada), and later by the icon of Mexican revolutionary nationalism: Lazaro Cardenas del Rio. In both cases, the import was politically motivated and kept in step with the readjustment and consolidation of colonial powers. In time, the different variants of Protestantism led to inculturation and gave place to popular mestizo Evangelicalisms, patrimonial in kind rather than strictly modern. The characteristics of evangelical fundamentalism implanted in Mexico since the 1930s are consistent with the characteristics of Pentecostal and neo-Pentecostal churches of Mexico City in which fieldwork was conducted.

4.1 Arrival of Protestantism to Mexico

4.1.1 First Arrival of Historical Protestants (1857-1936)

The context of the implant of Protestant Evangelicalism in Mexico were the Reformation and Intervention Wars between the years of 1858-1867 which started internally with the confrontation between the Liberal and the Conservative parties. The war began with the attempts of the Liberal Party to limit the power of the Catholic Church: Church-State separation, freedom of religion, secularization of cemeteries and of the civil registry, and prohibition of public displays of religious worship (Bastian 1990a). The Constitution of 1857 still set the Catholic religion as the official religion of Mexico. However, before its enactment two laws were passed under the Liberal governments of Alvarez and Comonfort: The Juarez Act of 1855, abolishing ecclesiastical and military privileges, and the Lerdo Act (Miguel's, brother of Sebastian) of 1856, which allowed to sell property of civil and ecclesiastical corporations in favor of government revenue (Sierra 2010).

After the promulgation of the Constitution of 1857 another law was dictated against the clergy, the Iglesias Act of 1857, which banned the collection of fees, parochial perquisites and tithes to the poor classes. This package of anti-Catholic laws, along with the newly enacted Constitution, led to a three year civil war. The Constitutional government in the hands of Juarez established in the port of Veracruz. His main concern was

> to prevent that the civil war would unleash an international conflict. This was extremely difficult for the case of nations which expressly recognized the reactionary government [the Conservative's], such as England, France and Spain, or which did not recognize anyone, as the United States (Sierra 2010, 136).

Facing threats of invasion by Spain, the United States finally decided to recognize the government of Juarez on April 6, 1859.

That same year, in October, the government of Juarez promoted a Catholic schism trying to separate the low from the high clergy, but found no echo (Sierra 2010, 166ff). Apparently, this attempt came in response to the signing of the Mon-Almonte Treaty with which the conservatives would restore diplomatic relations with Spain in exchange for loans, whose obligations would be charged to the constitutional government.[31]

In these circumstances the government of Juarez and the US government signed the McLane-Ocampo Treaty (December 14, 1859). The treaty granted the US free transit in perpetuity across the Isthmus of Tehuantepec, and even foresaw the passage of US troops through the northern territories to the ports of Guaymas and Mazatlan in exchange of an economic compensation (Sierra 2010, 184ff). Only the outbreak of the Civil/Secession War in the United States (1861-1865) prevented the ratification of the treaty by the US Senate.

The observation that the Mexican Reformation War, besides the involvement of the detailed internal interests, hid the eventual confrontation and readjustment of colonial powers, is something that is not entirely out of question. When in February of 1860 the troops of Miramon advanced against Veracruz, home to the Juarez government, there was only, in the opinion of Sierra,

> one chance against it: American warships also parked in the anchorage of Veracruz. And here it was where the leaders of the Reformation government brought out the consequences of the MacLane Treaty. At the bottom of that treaty there was an

---

[31] It is true that no clause in the treaty forsaw new loans. Even worse: the treaty recognized old Spanish economic claims and accepted with no conditions that Spain, France and England could establish compensations for the lives and property of Spaniards damaged in Mexico. Compare Sierra (2010, 174).

alliance, it was clear, as there was another alliance in the bottom of the Mon-Almonte Treaty. President Buchanan agreed with the treaty; Commander Turner did not have to wait any more: in case of danger for the government he had recognized, danger which came from abroad, he did not have to hesitate, he would help Juarez (Sierra 2010, 193-194).

Turner proceeded thus when on March 6, 1860 captured the "General Miramon" and "Marques de la Habana" ships, one Mexican and the other Spanish, which dismantled any serious attempt by the conservatives to seize the port of Veracruz.

In 1861, when the Civil/Secession War in the United States began, the sympathy of President Lincoln to the Juarez government could be explained by the following reasons:

> The criterion of the [US] Government was, to say, *secretly* favorable to us [Mexicans]. It was corrected by the characteristic circumstances of that situation; by fear, first, that the South acquired the alliance of Mexico, and later by the hatred of all new focus of European influence in America and, especially, in the immediate vicinity of the Union remade by the force of blood and gold (Sierra 2010, 308).

Two factors decided the foreign tripartite intervention (1862-1867) in the London Convention: an internal one (the suspension of payments on the foreign debt by Juarez government), and the other external (the defeat of the Union forces in the Battle of Bull Run by the secessionist states in the US Civil War) both in July 1861 (Sierra 2010, 330ff). And as important as these two factors, once the Intervention War broke, was Juarez's insistence to resist at any cost in light of the expected victory of the US military northern forces (Sierra 2010, 407ff).

The Liberal victory of 1867 on Maximilian of Augsburg and the Conservative Party, brought another Catholic schism attempt, promoted by some 50 religious anti-Catholic Reformation societies who followed the model of the Freemason lodges (Bastian 1990a).

When Juarez died in 1872, there were about 60 congregations of this type nationwide, characterized by an anti-Catholicism linked to local political struggles. Between 1873 and 1875, under President Sebastian Lerdo de Tejada, the anticlerical liberal policy was radicalized by making constitutional all previous Reformation laws, by expelling religious orders, and by establishing a strict control of religious practices by banning the external manifestations of the Roman Catholic faith. It is in these years when 20 American missionaries of various Protestant traditional denominations first arrived to Mexico (Methodist, Presbyterian and Congregational). So this is how they came in contact with existing Reformation associations:

> What is significant is that all religious leaders immediately agreed to become Protestant reformers in a type of arrangement, true modus vivendi, between foreign missionaries and Mexican leaders. While the former put their financial resources to build or buy temples, build schools and develop a press, the latter offered their religious networks. Therefore, the Protestant partnership model developed in continuity with the Reformation religious model, whose guidelines lay in the Masonic societies with

Mexican leaders who were interested in continuing their political struggle against the Catholic Church (Bastian 1990a, 136).

By 1876, the now Reformation-Protestant congregations summed up 129 in number. They had grown in regions with textile workers and miners, which offered similar services to those offered by benefit societies *–mutualidades–* (schools and savings, in addition to proper religious services). These congregations were similar in their organization to benefit societies and also to spiritualist societies, whose growth took place under Lerdo de Tejada:

> Composed by minorities, these associations had as a central feature to offer the individual guidelines and organizational models unrelated with the traditional organizational models largely associated with Catholicism... The contradiction between traditional practices (based on patterns of patrimonialist social control) and a Constitution imposed by a liberal minority and claimed by it in an utopian way, would weave the space in which a metaphysical liberalism of absolute respect for the law could develop, rooted, in part, in *juarismo* and, above all, in [the later] *lerdismo* (Bastian 1990a, 137).

An initial inculturation of Evangelicalism brought in by Lerdo de Tejada to Mexico, took place during the Porfiriato (1877-1910), as Protestant congregations grew from 129 in 1876 to 700 in 1910. By 1882 there were only over 40 000 Protestants, but by 1910 they had increased to 70 000 (in all, a very small percentage of the total population by then estimated in 15 million, less than 0.5%: ultraminorities at last). Between 1877 and 1911, Protestant congregations were established in central Mexico, where they were the successors of the Reformation religious societies, especially in Zitacuaro, Michoacan, and in the Huastecas of Hidalgo and San Luis Potosi.

Protestant societies also spread in states where there existed an antagonism between peripheral regions with demands of autonomy and capital cities' elites. This happened with Methodism in the northern mountains of Puebla and in the Valley of Atoyac in Tlaxcala, with Presbyterianism in the Tabasco Chontalpa, and with Congregationalism in western Chihuahua.

Protestantism also reached the cities of the north and center of the country in which children of ranchers and laborers participated in congregations and

> who, having enjoyed the educational services were now new professionals, especially school teachers, journalists and employees of commercial houses. Cities like the capital city of the Republic, Puebla, Pachuca, Guanajuato, San Luis Potosi, Chihuahua, Torreon, Saltillo and Monterrey were places of major secondary and theological Protestant rural schools, to which urban congregations were linked (Bastian 1990a, 142).

Faced with this radical liberalism now Protestant in kind,[32] a new liberalism of "conciliation" came into existence that had as its

---

[32] One must not ignore the similarity between spiritualist and Protestant societies with masonic lodges: "Both [spiritualist and Protestant societies] were quite similar to the lodges on their world conception, inspired by liberal principles and centered on the individual, who is the foundation of society, and on its anti-Catholicism fight linked to a religious worldview... With the Church-State confrontation, taken to its paroxysm during the liberal government of Sebastián Lerdo de Tejada (1872-1876), spiritualist and Protestant societies had been established as organizations which strengthened the radical liberal space and supported the action taken by lodges. It is significant that the Roman Catholic Church had always denounced the trilogy of lodges, Protestant and spiritualist

foundation philosophical Positivism, which led to the birth of the new Order and Progress Party, authoritarian in type, led by Porfirio Diaz. In particular, Protestants were opposed in two points to the new Order and Progress Party: to its policy of reconciliation with the Catholic Church, and to the idea that order and progress should prevail over the practice of democracy.

Diaz's conciliatory policy ignored the Reformation laws and allowed mutual services between his regime and Catholic bishops:

> This Catholic expansion can be measured by the creation of dioceses, the opening of seminars and the formation of new religious orders, while the old ones resumed their traditional activities. The set of measures taken [by Diaz] resulted in a vigorous Catholicism, whose renewed activity drew the attention of the radical liberals, notably in 1895 when the country was consecrated to the Virgin of Guadalupe, and in 1896, when the V Mexican Provincial Council was held. That same year Mexico received for the first time since the Reformation [Age], the visit of an apostolic nuncio in the person of Monsignor Averardi (Bastian 1990a, 148).

Apart from the press, masonic lodges and Protestant and spiritualist societies remained a stronghold of opposition to Diaz, despite the achieved control over many lodges with the creation in 1890 of the Great Symbolic Diet, of which Diaz was Great Teacher. In July 1895, independent liberal journalists led by Vicente Garcia Torres, Filomeno Mata and Daniel Cabrera, founded the Reformation and Constitutional Group. The main

---

societies, ever since the second half of the [nineteenth] century and, moreover, during the Porfiriato" (Bastian 1990b, 55-56).

feature of liberalism was its double opposition to the Catholic Church and to reelection.[33]

In 1914, with the Mexican Revolution already on its way and one year after the assassination of President Madero and Vice-President Pino Suarez, the first Pentecostal evangelical church was established in Mexico: the Iglesia Apostólica de la Fe en Cristo Jesus.[34] It was founded in Villa Aldama, Chihuahua, by a woman, Romana Valenzuela, who had got in touched two years earlier with the Azusa Street Mission in Los Angeles, California, and had converted to Evangelicalism. A few years later, by 1918, the Asambleas de Dios were established in Mexico.[35]

4.1.2 Arrival of Evangelical Fundamentalism to Mexico (1936-1979)

The second moment of impulse to Evangelicalism in Mexico began in the 1930s with the arrival of William Cameron Townsend (1896-1982) to Mexico. Townsend was founder of the Summer Institute of Linguistics (SIL). His most important antecedent was his missionary work in Guatemala between 1917 and 1932. Townsend had come to Guatemala as a missionary of the Bible

---

[33] These networks of anti-Catholic societies explain Madero's "spiritualism", as is notably pointed out by Bastian (1990b, 76 fn. 5).

[34] Compare Garma and Leatham (2004, 146-147).

[35] Preaching during the service of Asambleas de Dios held on September 7, 2014. For an equifinal observation of the emergence of Modern Pentecostalism refer back to the third chapter (in special footnote 22).

House in Los Angeles and soon after joined the Central American Mission founded in 1890 by the fundamentalist Cyrus Ingerson Scofield. While in Guatemala, Townsend translated the New Testament into the Cakchiquel language, a Mayan language variant (Aldridge 2012, 3ff; Stoll 1985, 41ff).

When Townsend arrived to Mexico he cultivated the friendship of Moises Saenz, promoter of secondary education and an evangelical himself, and especially that of President Lazaro Cardenas (1934-1940). The context of the founding of the SIL in Mexico in 1936[36] was the nationalist and anticlerical policy that followed the *Cristero* War of 1926-1929.[37] A central point of the alliance between American evangelical fundamentalism and the leaders of revolutionary nationalism were the still existing tensions between the nationalist government and the Catholic Church (Hartch 2006; 2014, 22ff), in addition to the pragmatism/ extreme opportunism practiced by Townsend through the years and which would determine the "doble face" of his organization.

---

[36] SIL's official webpage gives 1934 as its foundation date. Compare SIL International (2016).

[37] For Meyer (2013), the distant background to the Cristero conflict goes back to the liberal policies of the Bourbons which abolished ecclesiastical immunity. These policies determined church subordination to the Spanish Crown first, and to the rule of law and the Mexican State after the Independence. Church opposition to reforms is, as such, a very old phenomenon. Even the involvement of clergy in the Independence War could be read through this lens. During the Independence War, "for the first time in Mexican history, the church is accused of taking advantage of popular 'piety and obedience' in order to drag Mexicans into a fight using religious excuses. In 1820 Spanish government officials blamed the church for this. After 1821 and until 1938 accusations will be repeatedly made now this time by Mexican government officials" (Meyer 2013, 19).

In order to establish in Mexico, Townsend decided to provide the organization with a dual character: as "linguists" (Summer Institute of Linguistics, SIL) and as translators of Bibles to different indigenous languages (Wycliffe Bible Translators, WBT) (Stoll 1985 , 99ff; Aldridge 2012, 3ff). Thus, he could get both financial support from missionary organizations in the United States, presenting himself as translator of Bibles (WBT), and Mexico's government support, where his organization appeared as a scientific-linguistic and humanitarian enterprise (SIL).[38]

The missionary SIL-WBT model was the same one used by Hudson Taylor in the China Inland Mission in 1865 (Aldridge 2012, 3ff). This mission model ("faith missions") presupposed a "pre-millennial" eschatological doctrine, according to which the second coming of Jesus Christ should only occur after the Gospels were scattered across the globe in all existing languages. This kind of mission did not ask for donations but practiced financial independence: financial support was expected to appear miraculously in response to devout prayer.

---

[38] Townsend's immediate problem was to evangelize a country with an anticlerical government. In Hartch's (2006) opinion, in special chapters 2, 3 and 4, the way out of this problem was a non-orthodox alliance between evangelical fundamentalism and Cardenas government. This alliance tacitly agreed that Townsend would provide help in sowing an evangelical opposition to militant Catholicism by proselytizing through the SIL facade. On the other side, Cardenas would find in Townsend an ally in his policy of "integrating" native Mexico's population to the nation (the Ministry of Education would support SIL's linguists for decades). In addition, Cardenas found in Townsend a faithful publicist of his nationalist policies in the US, particularly the major government expropriation of oil industry in 1938.

The SIL-WBT missionary enterprise had also been preceded by the sanctifying Keswick teachings which emphasized a consacrated Christian life and spiritual exaltation for Christian service.[39] The result is that such missions were projected on the basis of exalted missionaries whom received no salary at all. The central concern of these missions was the salvation of souls, and to focus at efforts in evangelization rather than at educational or social activities. The proliferation of independent Bible institutes was in line with the growth of faith missions because they were expressly designed to infuse in missionaries a Keswick type spirituality –the promotion of practical sanctification in everyday life–, providing them with the minimum necessary biblical knowledge for a quick evangelization.

During its first years of existence, the Keswick Convention shaped what might be termed a distinctive charismatic theology (Brooke 1907, 75ff): a) first, sanctification by faith in Christ; b) then, the consecration by the Holy Spirit; and c) finally, the spread of the gospel to every corner of the planet (empowerment for mission). Or as put by Merino (2012, 576ff) in an attempt to systematize what would later be identified as Pentecostal theology: Christ saves, sanctifies, heals and will return (to which now one must add the Neo-Pentecostal emphasis: Christ also causes the betterment of

---

[39] Keswick is the name of a village in the county of Cumbria, in the northwest coast of England. For a history of the early years of the Keswick Convention –the first was held in 1875–, organized by an Anglican pastor, Thomas D. Harford-Battersby, and a Quaker, Robert Wilson, compare Harford (1907).

his faithful). Here it is worth highlighting the remarkable synchrony between the emergence of the new Pentecostal evangelical program and the successful spread of the British Empire on the planet.

Initially, faith missions served to feed missionary enterprises with denominational missionaries, although in the course of the twentieth century they became the dominant form of American missionary enterprise. What is described here is the progressive growth of evangelical fundamentalism, for whom the purpose of conversion is above a charitable view which emphasizes the social dimension of Christianity. For fundamentalist evangelism, Christianity is a unique religion in whose center is the evangelical doctrine.

Evangelical fundamentalism would boost Townsend's enterprise, which would consider herself as anti-modernist and ecclesiastically separatist. It would also emphasize doctrinal orthodoxy, biblical inerrancy and literalism, while endorsing creationism. In another definition, evangelical fundamentalism is characterized by the importance placed on conversion for salvation, on activism leading to the conversion of others, and in believing in biblical inerrancy and literalism and in the importance of the cross and the crucifixion of Christ to reconcile us with God.

SIL-WBT formalized its work in Mexico through agreements with the Ministry of Education, the first of which was signed in 1951 and whose consecutive renewal took place until 1979 (Hartch 2006, 77ff; 2014, 22), when the government of President Jose Lopez Portillo decided not to endorse the partnership agreement with SIL (though it did not ban its activities). The primary reason for this: it had been spread into news media a conspiracy theory accusing the SIL to serve US interests. The truth is that with the termination of the contract would also end SIL's indigenous image in Latin America (Stoll 1985, 289ff).

During the twentieth century, Townsend's project extended to several Latin American countries such as Peru (1946) and Colombia (1962), and reached global proportions when in 1953 arrived to the Philippines (Stoll 1985). By 1957, SIL was established in Vietnam and Cambodia, and also founded in 1956 one of its most successful subsidiaries in Papua New Guinea.

While Townsend's missionary enterprise could be considered as one of the most important American faith mission of the twentieth century (Aldridge 2012), it is also true that it had failures, many of which (the Philippines and Vietnam) made evident SIL's links with the United States Central Intelligence Agency (CIA) (Stoll 1985). SIL's operations spread to Asia and Africa, but encountered difficulties in India, with the expulsion of the Asia Foundation. Links were found between the Foundation and the CIA and, consequently, the Indian government banned all social science research with US funding. In Nepal it fared worse: they were expelled in 1976 (Stoll 1985, 343ff).

In 1982, when Stoll published his original English version, a summary table of the number of languages and SIL-WBT staff involved in missionary work, presented as an appendix of the book (Stoll 1985, 463), counted 925 languages studied by 4 512 evangelical missionaries (of whom 3 197 or 71% were US nationals). All that remains is amazement at the scale of a project that aims to bring the good news in all the world's languages. Could the same be said of the blindness of the fundamentalist evangelical enterprise which made it possible?

Everything seems to indicate that a conspiracy theory is simply untenable for many reasons: because the Mexican government supported the project for over 40 years, because the predominant evangelical denominations between missionaries and, presumably, among the first native evangelical communities were traditional (Methodists, Baptists, Presbyterians), and because SIL-WBT itself was rather reluctant to charismatic/ Pentecostal evangelism. Besides, Stoll argues that a conspiracy theory falls short when one is faced, in such inculturation undertakings, with the law of unintended consequences:[40] "Consider the religious genealogy of the Zapatista rebels in Chiapas, which can be traced back to the challenge that the SIL's Mayan converts posed to a still-colonial Catholic Church, forcing it to experiment with what became liberation theology" (Stoll 1996, 637).

---

[40] Put in words of Heinz von Foerster, social systems are non-trivial machines. Compare The Cybernetics Society (2010).

All this is very clear, but the suspicion remains given the evidence provided by the study that makes Townsend's apology. In 1967, Townsend managed to include SIL in the list of non-governmental organizations approved by the United States Agency for International Development (USAID). The US Congress increased funding for USAID had to do with the launch of the Alliance for Progress, an American program that sought social intervention in Latin America to inoculate the communist temptation, for example, by supporting adults literacy programs, field where SIL-WBT had proven experience through bilingual literacy among the indigenous population (Aldridge 2012, 232ff). SIL-WBT donations included not only those coming from the US government. During the 1950s to the late 1970s donations were also received through other sources, like those made by the Presbyterian oil tycoon, J. Howard Pew, of the Sun Oil Company, who was concerned about the effects that communism could bring on the free enterprise.

The same source provides information that allows the sound suspicion of an overrun of the organization by fundamentalist missionaries, more interested in spiritual exaltation than in scientific-linguistic work, to the point of stating that "there remained within the organization the ever-present threat of evangelistic activism and strains of anti-intellectualism undermining SIL's commitment to scholarship" (Aldridge 2012, 237). This in itself would suggest a suitable setting for SIL-WBT missionaries activism in areas with difficult access, and its likely involvement in insurgent activities... or, alternatively, in counter-insurgent intelligence operations.


4.2 Evangelical Fundamentalism in Pentecostal and Neo-Pentecostal Churches in Mexico City (2014-2015)


In this section we will show how and to what extent the traits of evangelical fundamentalism remain after 70 years of being implanted, and which managed to become hegemonic in most evangelical churches visited during fieldwork in 2014-2015. All churches showed signs of a conservative-fundamentalist social agenda, the only exception being the Lutheran Church, which has a social agenda with a progressist profile.[41]


4.2.1 Emphasis in Conversion


The importance of conversion is central to almost all the evangelical churches visited during fieldwork in the sense of the special and unique character of the evangelical doctrine and, therefore, of Christianity above other religions. For example, in

---

[41] The argument, of course, applies only to observations in the six evangelical churches visited in this study. These observations are not statistically representative, although it should be noted that the selection of churches intended a cross-section (two traditional denominational, three Pentecostal and one plain evangelical –they call themselves "*Compañerismo cristiano*"– which we considered as Neo-Pentecostal for its doctrinal features (theology of prosperity). Under-representation, if existent, took place with Para-Christian churches.

Centro Pentecostal Church one could hear the following testimony:

> God has done great things in my life and I have no way to pay
> Him back. I am grateful to my pastor, and to my brothers in prayer
> who have helped me grow. Sometimes we are in despair but things
> do not work this way, the Lord has His own tempo... For the glory
> of God, my brother (in blood) is now a member of this Church, as
> well as one of my neighbors. Another neighbor attended a single
> class in my house and that was enough, he decided to come to
> Church and was baptized here in the baptistery. May God bless
> you all and shall we continue growing![42]

Or the preaching on Luke 23, 1-25 given in Semilla de Mostaza Church:

> Black holes are unique in that as objects approach them there is a
> 'point of no return', a point beyond which it is impossible to
> overcome the attraction it exerts on things. Luke 23 shows us
> Pilate's point of no return in order to do what is correct with
> Jesus. You must consider that there might not be another chance
> for you to change your life and to repent... To consecrate oneself
> means surrendering completely to God. We should not study the
> Bible without having first a devoted heart. Herod also silenced
> God's voice in him. We must avoid doing the same with our lives.
> We must not only listen to God but to answer to his teachings and
> live our lives accordingly (even when I tweet wonderful things
> and write down in my Ipad)... If you are here for the first time, if
> you have not decided to offer your life to Jesus Christ, choose him
> up because no one ever before has overcome death... Herod ended
> up crazy and taking his own life. Christ died on my behalf to give
> me life ... We do not want your money, we want you to receive
> Christ... Today is the day of salvation if you decide well... Stand
> up if you choose well... It is a way of saying you trust Him your
> life... Applauses for those who are on their feet [those who stand
> are given a Bible as a gift].[43]

---

[42] Testimony during service celebrated in Centro Pentecostal Church, August 17, 2014.

[43] Preaching during service celebrated in Semilla de Mostaza Church, August 3, 2014.

Otherwise, Lutherans affirm ecumenism, the importance of inter-religious dialogue, and multiculturalism as central to their social agenda. During their services, they often spend time commenting social problems, such as unemployment and lack of opportunities for young people, and even violence in everyday life (days after the confrontation and death of an organized crime band with police forces and the Mexican Army in Tanhuato, Michoacan: "As Christians we must avoid violence and practice tolerance and peace instead",[44] or the poster stuck on one of the temple walls: "If you kill my race, by whom will my spirit speak?").

## 4.2.2 Active Differentiation from Pentecostal-Charismatic Choices

It is important to note that traditional denominational churches actively differentiate themselves from other Evangelical Pentecostal-charismatic options. For example, in the Iglesia Cristiana Remanente (Baptist) a brother said that Pentecostals made emphasis on the manipulation of emotion in order to get followers, but in reality much of what they believe had no biblical basis at all ("they interpret as is convenient for them, but they do not really have solid biblical studies").[45]

This does not mean they close their doors to former charismatic repentant seekers who wish to amend their mistakes. For example,

---

[44] Preaching during service in Cristo Church, May 24, 2015.
[45] Interview, August 23, 2014.

the case of a brother who had previously been charismatic pastor (Pentecostal), and had changed his predilection to Reformed Baptism. This brother had dissolved the church where he was pastor-leader because he realized he was cheating on his flock. One day he stood at the altar and told his faithful that there was no substance in the services they hold. In his view, deception was not about doing financial fraud but about not studying nor preaching the Word properly. Theology ultimately informs how worship is performed: there (with Pentecostals), worship is a time of praise and they only take 15 minutes for preaching, whereas here (with Baptists) is quite the opposite, we spend a lot more time studying the Word and its foundation.[46]

Also, the preaching on Deuteronomy 18, 9-22 in the Lutheran (Cristo) Church:

> Here [in this passage] we see the communities' concern with prophets' renewal. It does not happen as with some evangelical churches today, where they designate as prophet whomever gives them 50 000 pesos. These communities distinguish the prophet, who has a great status for the gift of prophecy, from the pastors, whom are not as important in front of them. Our community does not have these practices, however, we believe that the prophecy can come from anyone in the community.[47]

4.2.3 Biblical Literalism and Inerrancy

The most exceptional examples of biblical literalism and inerrancy come from the Asambleas de Dios (Assemblies of God). For

---

[46] Interview, March 22, 2015.
[47] Preaching during service in Cristo Church, February 1, 2015.

example, what was said in the Sunday Biblical School about Leviticus 18. The group dynamics was to write down on the blackboard the sexual prohibitions contained in this chapter and to look for other passages of scripture that referred to them. At least five sexual prohibitions were listed on the board: homosexuality, bestiality, adultery, polygamy and incest. Then the coordinator asked what did ordinary people think about the Bible, and wrote in the blackboard some possible answers: that people come up with disbelief when studying the Bible, that the Bible is the word of God, that the Bible is difficult to read because people do not understand it, etc. What does one thing have to do with the other?, he asked himself. He answered:

> God uses the Bible to restore our lives. And it does it against
> some of the laws in Mexico City as the one related to cohabitation
> societies, which allows for same sex marriages. It seems that in
> Mexico the message is: "As long as you are happy, do whatever
> you want". This happens because we do not defend the family.

A sister who participated in the biblical study group said that even though a person might have two sex organs, he/she should not be considered bisexual because "what is normal is to develop a single gender". Another sister added that psychiatrists at the UNAM (Universidad Nacional Autonoma de Mexico) "are in a great mistake because they no longer consider homosexuality a disease". Then the coordinator prevented everyone to visit places with the LGBT legend (Lesbian-Gay-Bisexual-Transgender) because they engage in sexual acts prohibited by the Bible. In his view, the world is corrupted especially by politics: "With these requirements [contained in Leviticus 18], God is taking us away from Mexico, not literally but in our private preferences. I think that everything is going to get worse and even persecution can take place against us".[48]

Another sign of biblical literalism and even of fundamentalism because it is related to provisions towards citizens' voting process on Election Day:

> The Bible says (1 Timothy 2) that requests, prayers, blessings and thanksgivings be made for all men, for kings and for all those in authority so that we may lead a peaceful and quiet life in all godliness and dignity, for this is good and acceptable before God our Lord... I hope, brethren, that you, if you have not exercised your right to vote, then go and vote after the service is finished. I was going to vote but there was a huge line and I really did not have time, but as soon as I finish here I will go... We must go [to vote], brothers, because that is the will of God; [if we do not vote] we do not have the right to complain... Of course, you should vote for the Lord's party [sic].[49] Watch, look in detail, pray, discuss, but we should exercise [our right]. Let's pray for both candidates and the authority, as for those who serve as authority in the electoral process, so the grace of God is poured over them. Father, this morning is our privilege and our responsibility to put in your hands the election process... We ask for your grace and blessing. Lord, you know who will govern... Pray for those states where there is violence: Chiapas, Guerrero, Oaxaca, Michoacan... We pray that your grace is poured. We ask that your Holy Spirit may be governing, moving across our Mexican nation. Please let everything we do may be guided by you...[50]

---

[48] Sunday Biblical School in Asambleas de Dios, March 1, 2015.

[49] Mexican Federal elections in 2015 saw the appeareance of a new national political party, Partido Encuentro Social (PES), which is identified with the social agenda of evangelical fundamentalism. In this sense, Pentecostal evangelical churches follow the trends of Latin American countries with significant presence of evangelical and Pentecostal population (Guatemala, Brazil, Peru, Chile, Colombia), and leads to the constitution of "evangelical blocs" in Congress. Compare Bastian (1999) and Gooren (2010).

[50] Preaching during the service of Asambleas de Dios Church on Federal Election Day, June 7, 2015.

As a counterpoint, it is worth to note here the opinion raised by the Lutheran (Cristo) Church on the same Federal elections. On that occasion, as part of the preaching to John 6: 1-15 (miracle of the multiplication of loaves), the Church's pastor passed very naturally from the biblical passage to Mexico's economic situation. She noted that this year, political elections would be held and, as we all have noticed on radio and TV, we are bombarded every single day with political propaganda. In her opinion, politicians make promises but forget them very easily as soon as they are favored by our vote. She introduced the issue of participation in elections and asked what the community thought about going to vote or refrain from doing so (cast a blank-invalid vote). She asked and gave the word to five parishioners. Everyone, without exception, was disillusioned with what was happening and doubted that any political party could change things. In general, the view was of discouragement and hopelessness. Someone even said that he had his IFE (Instituto Federal Electoral) voting card just because it was considered an official identification, but not because he had already make up his mind in favor of someone.[51]

4.2.4 Patriarchal-Patrimonial Leadership

In regard to gender relations, the Lutheran Church was the only one where the cult service was led by a woman pastor. In other churches women participated in various ministries (music —

---

[51] Preaching during service in Cristo Church, January 18, 2015.

usually waving flags and ribbons or playing tambourines, as
singers or soloists—, in the kitchen, welcoming and placing the
faithful in their seats —as *ujieres*—, etc.), but never in a
leadership position.[52] One could say that Pentecostal-charismatic
evangelical enterprises are patriarchal-patrimonial, unipersonal in
kind, where leadership and its replacement is a family-male
business, as is the case with Centro Pentecostal, Iglesia Cristiana
Centro de Convivencia, and to some measure with Semilla de
Mostaza.

The most notorious example of the patriarchal-patrimonial
character of *mestizo* evangelism –inculturated in a *Cristero* milieu
and which in time became a multinational enterprise–, is the Neo-
Pentecostal Church La Luz del Mundo, founded by a Mexican
migrant farm worker (*bracero*) named Aaron Joaquin Gonzalez in
1926 in the city of Guadalajara. He was succeeded after his death
in 1964 by his son Samuel Joaquin Flores, who after his death in
late 2014 was in turn succeeded by his son, Naason Joaquin
Garcia.[53] Compared to some modern neo-Hindu religious
movements, La Luz del Mundo falls short since the succession in
the lineage of Indian *gurus* at least manages to spare blood

---

[52] Women occupy a subordinate place in the Church and the world, and if anything, women
are considered the companion of a man of Christian virtues, exemplary householder and
successful in businesses. This is the case of some multinational neo-Pentecostal churches,
which make use of a coldly calculated marketing, as shown by Barreto (2015) in the case
of the Iglesia Universal del Reino de Dios, Brazilian in origin.

[53] Two newspaper references as a sample: Periodico El Universal (2014) and Periodico
Informador (2015).

relationships (it depends entirely on the candidate being an effective carrier of powers/ charismatic gifts).

## 4.2.5 Perseverance of the Rational-Liberal Model

Bastian (1992; 2006) has postulated two main theses in relation to Mexican and Latin American Pentecostalism:

a) The growth of evangelical groups of all kinds (traditional and Pentecostal) does not involve a reform of popular Catholicism nor an internal renewal of Protestantism, but a renewal of popular religion in the sense of a patch, acculturation,[54] of traditional denominational Protestantism to the practices and values of popular Catholicism.

b) Pentecostals are not only the most authentic product of this acculturation but even traditional denominational Protestantism has become pentecostalized, as with Presbyterians in southeastern Mexico (Yucatan and Chiapas).

These theses could very well be taken for good as long as one recognizes the persistence of the rational-liberal program of Christianity.

---

[54] We prefer to speak in this study of inculturation rather than acculturation. By inculturation is meant the mutual influence of two cultures in contact, in the sense of a second-order cybernetics. Acculturation refers more to a one-sided influence of the hegemonic culture over the subordinated one. For an explanation of the concept of second-order cybernetics refer to Vanderstraeten (2001).

How is this so? In the previous section the initial arrival and perseverance of evangelical ultraminorities was fully recognized. Their religious practices moved in the direction of a rational-liberal Christianity. Today they are best represented by the Lutheran Church, and mostly by the third largest religious group in Mexico, that of dissonant population (atheists or agnostics). This is confirmed by the main Mexican laboratory of religious change, the state of Chiapas,[55] which has been subjected in the last 150 years to several inculturation processes: Roman Catholic, evangelical traditional denominational (Presbyterian), Pentecostal, Catholic liberationist, and Catholic charismatic, phew! One should not forget that besides inculturation processes, Chiapas has also recently experienced an indigenous revolt (or is it that inculturation processes resulted in revolts?). Chiapas religious resonance is as follows: 58.3% Catholic, 27.4% evangelical and Para-Christian, 12.2% dissonant population (2.5 times the national average!) and 0.06% practice other religions.[56]

---

[55] Chiapas and Oaxaca concentrate the majority of Mexico's indigenous population, and also have the major number of municipalities where Catholic resonance is a minority. Indispensable research studies are those by Rivera et al. (2005) for Chiapas, and by Marroquin (2007) for Oaxaca.

[56] Refer back to section 2.1, second chapter.

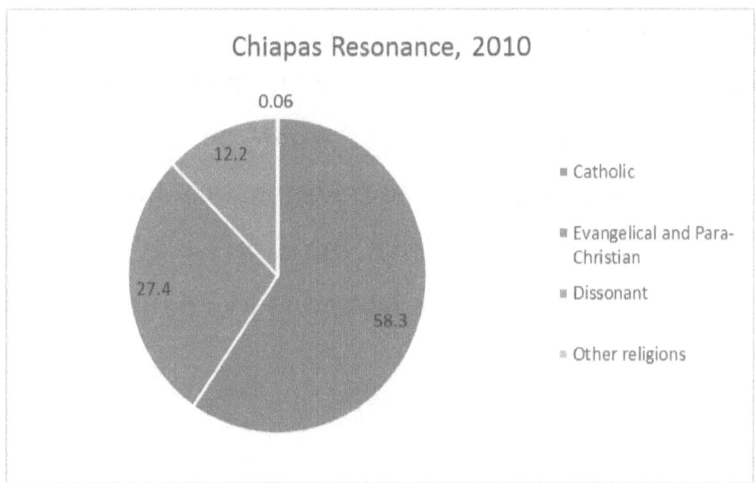


Along with rational-liberal evangelical groups and practicing minorities of other religions, it seems that the growing dissonant population could be primarily responsible for supporting social agendas related to ecumenism –and not to religious fundamentalism-exclusivism of any kind–, and to religious tolerance and literacy so necessary for the times we live in.

## 4.3 Conclusion

As has been observed by this reconstruction, the arrival of Protestantism to Mexico was driven by radical liberals in the last third of the nineteenth century, especially under President Sebastian Lerdo de Tejada. In those years, American missionary societies were invited to Mexico to oppose hegemonic Catholicism. These were mainly traditional Protestant denominational churches: Methodists, Presbyterians and Congregationalists. During the Porfiriato these societies were inculturated with masonic lodges and spiritualist societies prevalent in Mexico prior to their arrival, and altogether –lodges, spiritualist and Protestant societies– would be characterized by promoting religious opposition to traditional Catholicism and, politically, by refusing to postpone the exercise of substantive features of democracy (independent press and political parties, and effective elections).

In this first development it must be recognized a colonial factor at stake. The Liberal and Conservative parties in Mexico each lined up with the colonial powers in the country at that time. Conservatives lined up with Spain, France and England while Liberals favored the United States. The Mon-Almonte and the McLane-Ocampo treaties were expression of this alignment, and only showed the bankruptcy of public finances. So, the bet of radicals in favor of the unionist fraction of the Civil/Secession War in the United States, which in time proved fortunate, became a condition of possibility for the initial and relative successful implantation of Protestantism in Mexico.

The second impulse to Protestantism, now in a conservative and fundamentalist version, was launched during the Cardenas government in the 1930s and lasted for over 40 years. Cardenas support to SIL-WBT allowed to sow an opposition to a majority and militant Catholicism –the *Cristero* War had just finished–, while Townsend could clearly see the chance to spread the Gospel to the most remote regions in Mexico. What was relevant of these missions throughout the years was the missionary model used and which served as a basis for their missionary work: "fast track" conversions according to a catechesis which expressly emphasized charismatic features –practical sanctification in everyday life–, and that would eventually become in the twentieth century the predominant form of the American missionary enterprise.

The program of Evangelicalism which today represents the main opposition to Catholicism in Mexico, so called Pentecostalism, was developed during this second Protestant inculturation. For its development it can also be recognized a colonial factor at play: the Keswick Convention and the emergence within it, during the first years after its birth, of an organized evangelical communication oriented to world mission. This all happened in the context of the heyday and maximum power achieved by the British Empire worldwide.

Thus we come naturally to the realization of the features of Pentecostal evangelism –a true social policy– in most churches visited in Mexico City in the course of this research. They are in tune with evangelical fundamentalism: emphasis on activism that leads to conversion, rather than in charitable work which stresses the social dimension of Christianity. One could also distinguish an orthodox doctrinal focus which is characterized by creationism and biblical literalism and inerrancy. Christianity, evangelicals insistently repeat, is a unique religion in whose center is the evangelical doctrine. The cross and the crucifixion of Christ represent exclusive events that can reconcile us with God.

And here one must note again that all this happens in a context of modern sociocultural complexity. This means that the relations between religion and society are bearly durable and rarely definitive. Or in terms of the theory: the different emphases of the social agenda of evangelical churches studied are loosely coupled with all other communications, whichever they might be (economic, political, legal, scientific, etc.). Not all the faithful are fully identified with the doctrine, nor follow step by step the social agenda of the churches to which they belong. And even if they try to, they are at risk of being considered naive for consulting with their brethren in which bank is best to take a mortgage, or for doubting between doing prayer or taking birth control pills to prevent pregnancy, or finally for expecting to cure gastritis through the laying on hands practice.

# References

Aldridge Jr., Fredrick A. 2012. *The Development of the Wycliffe Bible Translators and the Summer Institute of Linguistics, 1934-1982*. Ph. D. Thesis, Department of History and Politics, School of Arts and Humanities. Stirling: University of Stirling.

Anderson, Allan H. 2014. The Emergence of a Multidimensional Global Missionary Movement: A Historical Review. In: *Pentecostal Mission and Global Christianity*, Ma, Wonsuk, Veli-Matti Kärkkäinen and J. Kwabena Asamoah-Gyadu (eds.), 10-25. Oxford: Oxford Center for Mission Studies.

Avalon, Arthur. 1950 [1918]. *The Serpent Power being the Shat-Chakra-Nirupana and Paduka-Panchaka. Two Works on Laya Yoga, Translated from the Sanskrit, with Introduction and Commentary*. Madras: Ganesh & Co.

Barreto J., Soraya. 2015. Who is the "Intelliman"? Ethos, Masculinity and Consumption in the IURD. Presentation at the *33rd. Biennial Conference of the International Society for the Sociology of Religion*, Catholic University of Louvain, Belgium, July 5, 2015.

Bastian, Jean Pierre. 2006. De los protestantismos históricos a los pentecostalismos latinoamericanos: Análisis de una mutación religiosa. *Revista de Ciencias Sociales (CI)-Universidad Arturo Prat* (16): 38-54.

Bastian, Jean Pierre. 1999. Los nuevos partidos políticos confesionales evangélicos y su relación con el Estado en América Latina. *Estudios sociológicos* 17 (49): 153-173.

Bastian, Jean Pierre. 1992. *La mutación de los protestantismos en América Latina. Una perspectiva socio-histórica*. México: Instituto Mexicano de Doctrina Social Cristiana (IMDOSOC), Colección Diálogo y autocrítica, No. 30.

Bastian, Jean Pierre. 1990a. Las sociedades protestantes y la oposición a Porfirio Díaz en México, 1877-1911. In: *Protestantes, liberales y francmasones: sociedades de ideas y modernidad en América Latina, siglo xix*, Bastian, Jean-Pierre (comp.), 132-164. México: CEHILA/ Fondo de Cultura Económica.

Bastian, Jean Pierre. 1990b. El impacto regional de las sociedades religiosas no católicas en México. *Relaciones* 11 (42): 49-78.

Battersby Harford, John. 1907. The Keswick Mission Council. In: *The Keswick Convention. Its Message, Its Method and Its Men*, Harford, Charles F. (ed.), 143-155. London: Marshall Brothers.

Brooke, Hubert. 1907. The Message. Its Method of Presentation. In: *The Keswick Convention. Its Message, Its Method and Its Men*, Harford, Charles F. (ed.), 75-86. London: Marshall Brothers.

Burke, Peter. 2010. *Hibridismo cultural. Reflexiones sobre teoría e historia*. Madrid: Akal.

De la Torre, Renée and Cristina Gutiérrez Z. (coords.). 2007. Territorios de la diversidad religiosa hoy. In: *Atlas de la diversidad religiosa en México*, 35-37. México: El Colegio de Jalisco/ El Colegio de la Frontera Norte/ CIESAS/ El Colegio de Michoacán/ Secretaría de Gobernación/ Universidad de Quintana Roo.

De la Torre, Renée and Eric Janssen. 2007. Ubicación y patrones de distribución. In: *Atlas de la diversidad religiosa en México*, 124-136. México: El Colegio de Jalisco/ El Colegio de la Frontera Norte/ CIESAS/ El Colegio de Michoacán/ Secretaría de Gobernación/ Universidad de Quintana Roo.

Dirección General de Asociaciones Religiosas (Secretaría de Gobernación). 2014. *Asociaciones religiosas por tradición al 2 de mayo de 2014*. www.asociacionesreligiosas.gob.mx/es/AsociacionesReligiosas/Numeralia (May 20, 2014).

Dirección General de Asociaciones Religiosas (Secretaría de Gobernación). 2014. *Ministros de culto registrados al 2 de mayo de 2014*. www.asociacionesreligiosas.gob.mx/es/AsociacionesReligiosas/Numeralia (May 20, 2014).

Dirección General de Asociaciones Religiosas (Secretaría de Gobernación). 2007. *Distribución de ministros registrados por credo religioso*. http://www.asociacionesreligiosas.gob.mx (September 3, 2007).

Dyer, Helen S. 192?. *Pandita Ramabai. Her Vision, Her Mission and Triumph of Faith*. Glasgow: Pickering & Inglis.

Dyer, Helen S. 1900. *Pandita Ramabai. The Story of her Life*. London: Morgan & Scott.

Eliade, Mircea and Ioan P. Couliano. 1992. *Diccionario de las religiones*. Barcelona: Paidós.

Farquhar, JN. 1915. *Modern Religious Movements in India*. New York: MacMillan.

Garma Navarro, Carlos. 2007. El pentecostalismo. In: *Atlas de la diversidad religiosa en México*, 79-84. México: El Colegio de Jalisco/ El Colegio de la Frontera Norte/ CIESAS/ El Colegio de Michoacán/ Secretaría de Gobernación/ Universidad de Quintana Roo.

Garma Navarro, Carlos. 1999. La situación legal de las minorías religiosas en México: balance actual, problemas y conflictos. *Alteridades,* 9 (18): 135-144.

Garma Navarro, Carlos and Alberto Hernández. 2007. Los rostros étnicos de las adscripciones religiosas. In: *Atlas de la diversidad religiosa en México*, 203-226. México: El Colegio de Jalisco/ El Colegio de la Frontera Norte/ CIESAS/ El Colegio de Michoacán/ Secretaría de Gobernación/ Universidad de Quintana Roo.

Garma, Carlos and Miguel Leatham. 2004. Pentecostal Adaptations in Rural and Urban Mexico: An Anthropological Assessment. *Mexican Studies/ Estudios Mexicanos* 20 (1): 145-166.

Gooren, Henri. 2010. The Pentecostalization of Religion and Society in Latin America. *Exchange* 39: 355-376.

Gutiérrez Z., Cristina. 2007. El protestantismo histórico. In: *Atlas de la diversidad religiosa en México*, 50-60. México: El Colegio de Jalisco/ El Colegio de la Frontera Norte/ CIESAS/ El Colegio de Michoacán/ Secretaría de Gobernación/ Universidad de Quintana Roo.

Gutiérrez Z., Cristina and Renée de la Torre. 2007. Otras evangélicas. In: *Atlas de la diversidad religiosa en México*, 92-97. México: El Colegio de Jalisco/ El Colegio de la Frontera Norte/ CIESAS/ El Colegio de Michoacán/ Secretaría de Gobernación/ Universidad de Quintana Roo.

Harford, Charles F. (ed.). 1907. *The Keswick Convention. Its Message, Its Method and Its Men*. London: Marshall Brothers.

Hartch, Todd. 2014. *The Rebirth of Latin American Christianity*. Oxford: Oxford University Press.

Hartch, Todd. 2006. *Missionaries of the State. The Summer Institute of Linguistics, State Formation, and Indigenous Mexico, 1935-1985*. Tuscaloosa: University of Alabama Press.

Henke, Frederick G. 1909. The Gift of Tongues and Related Phenomena at Present Day. *The American Journal of Theology* 13 (2): 193-206.

Hernández H., Alberto. 2007. El cambio religioso en México: crecimiento y auge del pentecostalismo. In: *Más allá del espíritu. Actores, acciones y prácticas en iglesias pentecostales*, Rivera F., Carolina and Elizabeth Juárez C. (eds.), 53-90. México: CIESAS/ El Colegio de Michoacán.

Instituto Nacional de Estadística y Geografía (INEG). 2014. *Aspectos metodológicos de cuestionarios censales*. México: INEG. http://www.inegi.org.mx/est/contenidos/proyectos/aspectosmetodologicos /cuestionarios/default.aspx (June 10, 2014).

Instituto Nacional de Estadística y Geografía (INEG). 2011. *Panorama de las religiones en México 2010*. México: INEG.

Instituto Nacional de Estadística, Geografía e Informática (INEGI). 2005. *La diversidad religiosa en México. XII Censo general de población y vivienda 2000*. México: INEGI.

Kavan, Heather. 2004. Glossolalia and Altered States of Consciousness in Two New Zealand Religious Movements. *Journal of Contemporary Religion* 19 (2): 171-184.

Kosambi, Meera. 1992. Indian Response to Christianity, Church and Colonialism. Case of Pandita Ramabai. *Economic and Political Weekly* 27 (43-44): 61-70.

Kripananda, Swami. 1995. *The Sacred Power: A Seeker's Guide to Kundalini*. South Fallsburg: SYDA Foundation.

Luhmann, Niklas. 2009. *Sociología de la religión*. México: Herder/ Universidad Iberoamericana (UIA).

Luhmann, Niklas. 2007a. *La sociedad de la sociedad*. México: Herder/ UIA.

Luhmann, Niklas. 2007b. *La religión de la sociedad*. Madrid: Trotta.

Luhmann, Niklas. 2005. *El arte de la sociedad*. México: Herder/ UIA.

Luhmann, Niklas. 2002. *El derecho de la sociedad*. México: UIA.

Luhmann, Niklas. 1998. *Sistemas sociales. Lineamientos para una teoría general*. Barcelona: Anthropos/ UIA/ Centro Editorial Javeriano.

Luhmann, Niklas. 1996. *La ciencia de la sociedad*. México: UIA/ ITESO/ Anthropos.

Luhmann, Niklas. 1989. *Ecological Communication*. Chicago/ Cambridge: The University of Chicago Press/ Polity Press.

Maier, Elizabeth. 2006. Tránsitos territoriales e identidad de las mujeres indígenas migrantes. *Papeles de población* 12 (47): 201-225.

Marroquín, Enrique. 2007. *El conflicto religioso. Oaxaca 1976-1992*. México: UNAM-CIICH/UABJO-IIS.

May, L. Carlyle. 1956. A Survey of Glossolalia and Related Phenomena in Non-Christian Religions. *American Anthropologist* 58 (1): 75-96.

Merino B., Patricio. 2012. Contenidos teológicos para un diálogo católico-pentecostal. Hacia un testimonio común del evangelio. *Teología y vida* 53 (4): 575-602.

Meyer, Jean. 2013. *La cristiada. Vol. 2. El conflicto entre la iglesia y el Estado*. México: Siglo XXI editores.

Mukti Prayer-Bell. 1906 (September). Kedgaon: Mukti Mission Press. http://www.google.com.mx/url?sa=t&rct=j&q=&esrc=s&source=web&cd=1&cad=rja&uact=8&ved=0CB4QFjAA&url=http%3A%2F%2Fimageserver.library.yale.edu%2Fdigcoll%3A210150%2F500.pdf&ei=m-VzVLDXEYGmyATdioHICA&usg=AFQjCNH00IR_exc5uiRJNMRK79HgEa_f_g&bvm=bv.80185997,d.aWw (December 14, 2018).

Naselli, Andrew D. 2008. Keswick Theology: A Survey and Analysis of The Doctrine of Sanctification in The Early Keswick Movement. *Detroit Baptist Seminary Journal* (13): 17-67.

Orellana U., Luis A. 2016. La matriz religiosa del pentecostalismo en Chile: la Iglesia Metodista Pentecostal y la Iglesia Evangélica Pentecostal (1909-1973). *Memoria y Sociedad*, 20 (40): 266-285.

Ornelas, Marco. 2018a. El don de lenguas como kriya: la conexión hinduista. *Revista Cultura & Religión* 12 (1): 97-114.

Ornelas, Marco. 2018b. *Modern Religious Differentiation: The Latin Mass (1517-1570)*. Mexico: Self-Published. https://www.amazon.com/dp/1790664047 (December 14, 2018).

Ornelas, Marco. 2015. *Evangelismo defeño: Reporte de campo, 2014-2015 (30 de noviembre de 2015)*. https://www.academia.edu/19377529/EVANGELISMO_DEFENO_REPORTE_DE_CAMPO_2014-2015 (December 14, 2018).

Periodico El Universal. *Hijo de Samuel Joaquín, nuevo líder de La Luz del Mundo*. http://archivo.eluniversal.com.mx/estados/2014/asume-nuevo-lider-de-iglesia-la-luz-del-mundo--1061935.html (January 7, 2016).

Periodico Informador. *Dan bienvenida a la Santa Convocación*. http://www.informador.com.mx/jalisco/2015/608007/6/dan-bienvenida-a-la-santa-convocacion.htm (January 7, 2016).

Piedra S., Arturo. 2000. *Evangelización protestante en América Latina. Análisis de las razones que justificaron y promovieron la expansión protestante, 1830-1960. Tomo 1*. Quito: Consejo Latinoamericano de Iglesias (CLAI).

Prieto, Mercedes et al. 2006. Respeto, discriminación y violencia: Mujeres indígenas en Ecuador, 1990-2004. In: *De lo privado a lo público: 30 años de lucha ciudadana de las mujeres en América Latina*, Lebon, Nathalie and Elizabeth Maier (comps.), 158-180. México: LASA/ UNIFEM/ Siglo XXI.

Ramabai, Pandita. 1901 [1887]. *The High-Caste Hindu Woman*. New York: Fleming H. Revell Company.

Rivera F., Carolina, et al. 2005. *Diversidad religiosa y conflicto en Chiapas. Intereses, utopías y realidades*. México: UNAM-IIFL/ PROIMMSE/ CIESAS.

Robeck, Cecil M. Jr. 2014. The Origins of Modern Pentecostalism: Some Historiographical Issues. In: *The Cambridge Companion to Pentecostalism*, Robeck, Cecil M. Jr. and Amos Yong (eds.), 13-30. Cambridge: Cambridge University Press.

Sierra, Justo. 2010 [1905]. *Juárez: su obra y su tiempo*. México: Porrúa.

SIL International. 2016. *Our History*. http://www.sil.org/about/history (December 14, 2018).

Stichweh, Rudolf. 2015. Comparing Systems Theory and Sociological Neo-Institutionalism. Explaining Functional Differentiation. In: *From Globalization to World Society. Neo-Institutional and Systems Theoretical Perspectives*, Holzer, Boris, Fatima Kastner and Tobias Werron (eds.), 23-36. New York/ London: Routledge.

Stichweh, Rudolf. 2011. Niklas Luhmann. In: *The Wiley-Blackwell Companion to Major Social Theorists, Vol. II Contemporary Social Theorists*, Ritzer, George and Jeffrey Stepnisky (eds.), 287-309. Chichester: Wiley-Blackwell.

Stichweh, Rudolf. 2008. The Eigenstructures of World Society and the Regional Cultures of the World. In: *Frontiers of Globalization Research. Theoretical and Methodological Approaches*, Rossi, Ino (ed.), 133-149. New York: Springer.

Stoll, David. 1996. Missionaries and Foreign Agents. *American Anthropologist* 98 (3): 636-638.

Stoll, David. 1985. *¿Pescadores de hombres o fundadores de imperio? El Instituto Lingüístico de Verano en America Latina*. Lima: Centro de Estudios y Promoción del Desarrollo (DESCO).

Torres Nafarrate, Javier. 2004. *Luhmann: la política como sistema*. México: Fondo de Cultura Económica/ Facultad de Ciencias Políticas y Sociales de la UNAM/ UIA.

The Cybernetics Society. 2010. *Heinz von Foerster*. http://www.cybsoc.org/heinz.htm (December 14, 2018).

Wilkinson, Michael. 2015. The Emergence, Development, and Pluralisation of Global Pentecostalism. In: *Handbook of Global Contemporary Christianity: Themes, and Developments in Culture, Politics, and Society*, Hunt, Stephen (ed.), 93-112. The Netherlands: Brill.

Vanderstraeten, Raf. 2001. Observing Systems: A Cybernetic Perspective on System/ Environment Relations. *Journal for the Theory of Social Behavior* 31 (3): 297-311.